ACTIVITY ACCOUNTING

THE WILEY/NATIONAL ASSOCIATION OF ACCOUNTANTS PROFESSIONAL BOOK SERIES

ACTIVITY ACCOUNTING

AN ACTIVITY-BASED COSTING APPROACH

JAMES A. BRIMSON
Coopers & Lybrand, Deloitte

JOHN WILEY & SONS, INC.

New York • Chichester • Brisbane • Toronto • Singapore

Library of Congress Cataloging-in-Publications Data:

Brimson, James A., 1947-
    Activity accounting : an activity-based costing approach / by James A. Brimson.
        p.   cm. – (The Wiley/National Association of Accountants professional book series)
    Includes index.
    ISBN 0-471-53985-6
    1. Cost accounting. 2. Computer integrated manufacturing systems-
-Evaluation. I. Title. II. Series.
HF5686.C8B674 1991   90-21506
657'.42–dc20

Printed in the United States of America

10 9 8 7

CONTENT

ACKNOWLEDGMENTS

No book is solely the effort of its author. This book is certainly no exception, and credit must be given to all those who have commented, reviewed, and provided technical assistance during the various stages of its development.

I would like to give special thanks to Professors George Foster of Stanford University, Michael Bromwich of the London School of Economics, John Antos of the University of Dallas and Alfred King of the National Association of Accountants, for their input in reviewing and commenting on the contents of this book.

I am also grateful for the support I have received from the consultants and support staff in the Coopers & Lybrand Deloitte office in London whose experience and knowledge of activity-based costing have helped bring this book to its overall shape. The Wiley editorial and production team must be acknowledged for their professionalism and patience in bringing this book to press; special thanks go to Erika Heilman, Linda Indig and her team.

I am indebted to my colleagues Callie Berliner, Tom Pryor, and Mike Roberts, who have been very influential in shaping the current state of cost management thinking. Finally, I must thank those special people, Carolyn Brimson, Ellen Kadin, Maxine Flax, and my family, Jimmy and Katy, for all the support and inspiration they have provided.

PREFACE

Never in the history of accounting has an idea such as activity accounting, or activity-based costing (ABC), moved so quickly from concept to implementation. One individual can take a great deal of credit for this transformation. Jim Brimson was in at the beginning of ABC when he was associated with Computer Aided Manufacturing—Internationl (CAM-I). His work there, with a group of executives from some 40 forward-looking organizations, culminated in an award-winning book, coauthored with Callie Berliner, *Cost Management for Today's Advanced Manufacturing: The CAM-I Conceptual Design* (Harvard Business School Press, 1988). That book represented the best thinking of the CAM-I task force, but there is no doubt in my mind that Jim Brimson deserves a lot of the credit for pushing the CAM-I project through to completion. Many of the *ideas* expounded in that book are now being brought into *practice* in Mr. Brimson's current volume, *Activity Accounting: An Activity-Based Costing Approach*.

In this book, the author identifies a number of benefits to be derived from activity accounting. Most important among these, in my opinion, are:

- Improving make/buy, estimating, and pricing decisions that are based on a product cost that mirrors the manufacturing process
- Facilitating elimination of waste by providing visibility of non–value added activities
- Linking corporate strategy to operational decision making
- Encouraging continual improvement and total quality control because planning and control are directed at the process level
- Improving the effectiveness of budgeting by identifying the cost/performance relationship of different service levels
- Improving profitability by monitoring total life-cycle cost and performance
- Providing insight into the fastest-growing and least visible element of cost—overhead

If this book helps you accomplish only one or two of these objectives, it will provide a quantum leap in corporate performance. Accomplishing all of them will put a firm into the world-class league.

After two introductory chapters, which lay the framework for understanding activity accounting and its relationship to the changing global marketplace, the book jumps into one of the basic issues facing financial and operating managers: Just what is an activity, what does activity accounting provide, and how does it fit in as part of the more global approach now being referred to as a "cost management system." The term *cost driver* is being used more and more in business, both in manufacturing and in service organizations. In an effort to relate cause and effect—in other words, to try to understand why costs are incurred and what they accomplish—Chapters 3 and 4 provide an important framework for understanding these concepts.

The present cost accounting systems, used by most U.S. organizations, have been developed over a 50-year period. They do a very good job of providing inventory costs for financial statement purposes, but business decisions are rarely made utilizing balance sheet information. Operating and line managers need current information that is relevant to a specific purpose. General purpose financial statements fail that test. Activity analysis provides a much better framework for understanding how and why costs are incurred. Once you look at a business in terms of activities, a lot of other things fall into place. Chapter 5 provides a thorough discussion of activity analysis.

Chapters 6 and 7 then provide the background fundamentals for Chapters 8 and 9, which are the heart of the book. These two chapters distinguish this volume from almost everything else that has been written on the subject. Mr. Brimson gives explicit, detailed instructions on calculating an activity cost and then tracing relevant cost drivers to ultimate business uses. Readers with a good background in ABC could immediately go to Chapters 8 and 9, but for most people starting at the beginning of the book will probably be necessary.

This volume is not light reading. Mr. Brimson does not provide an "easy answer" or any "instant solutions." What he proposes for you, the reader, is actually revolutionary. Throwing over the old accounting regime and installing a new regime will be resisted by many accountants. The *users* of accounting data, however, are beginning to vote with their PCs. If accountants do not provide relevant and useful information, as contrasted with reams of accounting data, then engineers, production supervisors, and marketing managers will develop their own ways of looking at and analyzing what is happening. As surely as the sun rises every morning in the East, if users each develop their own mini-MIS approach, chaos will follow. Organizations can have only one cost-accounting system, and it should be run by accountants. Over the next five years, cost management systems will undoubtedly be based on activity analysis, activity costs, and cost drivers.

Only accountants can provide a cohesive framework that is truly responsive to the multiple information needs of a business. Mr. Brimson, in this volume, shows how to develop and implement that framework. Now it is up to you, the reader, to "make it happen."

ALFRED M. KING

National Association of Accountants
February 1991

ACTIVITY ACCOUNTING AND ENTERPRISE EXCELLENCE

The purpose of this chapter is to:

- Describe the role of activity accounting in achieving enterprise excellence
- Describe the conventional approach to **cost** accounting
- Provide an overview of activity accounting
- Contrast conventional **cost accounting systems** with activity accounting
- Describe the role of activity accounting in the management process
- Describe the benefits of activity accounting

EXCELLENCE CANNOT BE BUILT ON A WEAK FOUNDATION

The business world has undergone a major transformation in recent years. Today **customers** expect products with high **quality**, expanded functionality, and low price. These expectations are a consequence of unprecedented scientific and technological progress coupled with global competitors who coerce other companies in an industry to adopt a strategy of enterprise excellence or be forced out of business. Competition can quickly turn market supremacy into oblivion.

To remain competitive it is crucial for companies not to become complacent. Too often businesses consider themselves to be invulnerable and consequently implement a strategy of exploiting their current market position. However, proprietary advantage never lasts. An attempt to keep profit margins stable by increasing price inevitably results in an erosion of market position. The reason for this is that the fundamental factors driving cost and performance are not addressed by such a strategy.

As products mature, competition increases, and prices and margins inevitably decline as they succumb to competitive pressures. The introduction of new, innovative products by competitors lessens the image advantage of the earliest companies, and prices become increasingly important in buying decisions. As a consequence, companies must constantly enhance product functionality, improve productivity, and reduce costs. However, most companies use current-period profitability as a barometer of success and do not make the fundamental changes until competitive pressures force the change.

With the squeeze in profit margins come the inevitable short-term approaches to cost reduction:

- Freeze hiring
- Freeze overtime and pay increases
- Freeze nonessential travel
- Early retirement
- Cut back R&D and investment
- Downsize

These approaches may ease short-term cash flow problems but, in the long run, hurt company performance and alienate customers. Too often companies drive some of their best employees to competitors, and those that remain are overburdened and unhappy. This fosters an organization whose members are so anxious about protecting their jobs that they become risk averse.

Rather than implement short-term fixes, companies must (1) address the fundamental problems and eliminate nonproductive structured cost; (2) design cost out of products, activities, and business processes; and (3) greatly improve efficiencies in the long run. The key is to manage and reduce the work load—not just the work force—and to streamline the activities of the remaining work load. In other words, it is essential that an enterprise continually improve the way it manufactures, sells, and manages its activities (work).

The hallmark of enterprise excellence is a continual commitment to being globally competitive. This requires the never-ending elimination of waste as well as the ability to maintain industry leadership in introducing profitable new products or product variations. The most visible manifestations of successful manufacturers in this new **environment** are increased automation and computerization, reduced levels of direct labor and inventory, increased attention to product and production **planning**, and shorter product life cycles. The revolution is based on new **manufacturing** philosophies such as **just-in-time (JIT)**, **total quality management (TQM)**, and manufacturing resource planning (MRPII), along with judicious implementation of advanced technologies.

Many managers have confused these tools and techniques with the actual achievement of excellence. It is easy to blame failing competitiveness on a technology void rather than a management void. Manufacturing techniques such as JIT and TQM are not the sole requirements for competitiveness; they are merely prerequisites. A recent visit to a multinational company illustrates this point. The company pointed proudly to a division that produced VCR tapes. The division had implemented JIT, TQM, MRPII, and other manufacturing techniques resulting in dramatic productivity improvements. Productivity had steadily improved with the same level of expenditures:

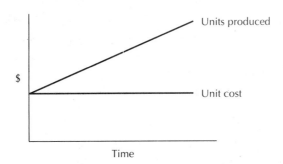

However, in spite of the dramatic productivity improvements, profitability had remained unchanged because the sales price of VCR tapes had steadily decreased during the same period. *All* companies in the industry were excellent. The manufacturing improvements were the price the division had to pay to remain in business in this very competitive industry. The marketplace had enforced manufacturing excellence.

This is not to suggest that JIT, TQM, MRPII, and other advanced technologies are not important. To the contrary, they are irrevocably intertwined with a company's quest for greater competitiveness. The challenge is to perform all activities correctly the *first time*. This requires getting the workers involved directly in fixing the causes of the problems through programs such as just-in-time and total quality management.

However, competitive advantage accrues to those companies that use manufacturing excellence as a proactive rather than a reactive strategy. Long-term profitability is determined by the advantages or disadvantages relative to competitors. Companies that eliminate waste and strive for absolute quality in all aspects of management before competitors do can use the increased revenue to invest in R&D, reinvest in improving company activities, lower cost, or build a strong cash liquidity position. The companies who achieve these results will be in a position to dictate the basis of competition in their industry.

To stay ahead of the competition, companies must have information to provide the necessary understanding of the factors they can influence. Management must place unrelenting pressure on the entire organization for measurable cost reduction and productivity gains. Vigilance is critical because it is difficult to regain cost competitiveness once it is lost. Costs must not be allowed to get out of line in the first place.

An important reason a company's costs become noncompetitive is that conventional cost accounting systems distort product costs and do not highlight productivity improvement opportunities, thus leading to poor decisions. Most managers routinely make critical decisions without the facts. They ignore what Napoleon meant when he said "God is on the side of the army with the biggest battalions" and are thus vulnerable to serious problems. In other words, companies that have relevant and timely information have a much greater chance of making successful decisions.

Competitive advantage demands that companies be able to provide accurate answers to the following questions:

1. What are the influenceable (and directly traceable) costs and profits for each major product line and customer?
2. What are the cost behavior patterns of each activity, including its **capacity**, and how much can volume be increased or decreased before costs change?
3. What is the waste (non–value-added) component of cost, and what are the best practices for an activity?
4. How does **overhead cost** vary with changes in business? What costs are avoidable if volume declines?
5. How do the **current cost** structure, capacity utilization, and nonfinancial performance trends compare with those of competitors?
6. How can low cost be designed into new and existing products?

Cost management based on this sort of activity information is the heart of the new management information systems that help managers answer these critical questions. Activity accounting profiles a company in terms of the cost and performance of its specific activities.

ENTERPRISE EXCELLENCE

Enterprise *excellence* is the cost-effective integration of activities within all units of an organization to continuously improve the delivery of products and **services** that satisfy the customer. A manufacturing enterprise structured to exploit market and technical opportunities will achieve a competitive advantage. The ability to achieve and sustain enterprise excellence requires the deliberate and continuous improvement of *all* activities—not just manufacturing—within an enterprise, including research, design, development, marketing, finance, production, packaging, logistic support, retirement, and disposal. The key elements of manufacturing excellence are discussed in this section.

Cost-effectiveness

Activities should be accomplished as cost-effectively as possible. This means the company is a low-cost producer but not necessarily the lowest-cost producer. Being low cost means one's total costs are below the average of all competitors offering equivalent products or services to the same customer segments. The position of lowest-cost producer, is, however, sometimes achieved to the detriment of quality, service, employee satisfaction, and investment in the future.

Often companies compete on bases other than cost—such as rapid new product introduction, quality, and field service. However, once a competitive strategy has been defined, the activities should be structured to be as cost-effective as possible. Anything else results in *waste*.

Integration of Activities

Understanding of company and departmental objectives must be diffused. Companies are organized and managed with rigid topical specialization. Management reporting emphasizes individual organizational units almost as if they were independent, self-contained disciplines. Costs incurred in one department are impacted by decisions and outputs from other departments. Under the traditional structure of responsibility accounting, the interrelationship of activities among departments is ignored. This practice is in conflict with the concept of the unified enterprise.

This separation of organizational responsibility is dysfunctional because it encourages competition among departments and provides limited incentive to take action that hinders a department's performance but is in the best interest of the company. As a consequence, in many companies, the engineers view manufacturing and marketing as "the enemy." The financial people often take the attitude that they are the "watchdogs" trying to catch other members of management when they are wrong. The key is to direct the attention of the organization to the *real* competition so that they can concentrate their energies on other firms rather than compete against one another.

The importance of understanding interdependencies of activities is compounded in an advanced manufacturing environment. Today companies are implementing integrated manufacturing systems and other advanced technologies in order to achieve a harmonious flow of materials, tools, parts, and information through the factory. Integrated systems tear down the barriers between departments and involve getting information and ideas from everyone in the organization and putting them to work.

Coherence within All Units of an Organization

Coherence must be based on actions (activities), not hierarchies. Enterprise excellence requires involvement of all units, not just production. The role of the finance department is, for example, to provide meaningful data in a format conducive to decision making. This role is just as critical to achieving enterprise excellence as are the manufacturing functions. Similarly, the streamlining of the customer order process is as critical as are quick production cycles.

Continual Improvement

Enterprise excellence requires continual improvement in all enterprise activities—there is no room for complacency. This requires managing activities so as to minimize waste and non–value adding activities and constantly striving for perfection in all areas of the business.

Delivery of Products and Services

Products and services are where the business enterprise and the marketplace meet. Product design must exploit the market opportunities within the strategic framework. But it must balance the exploitation of market opportunities with the facilitation of low-cost manufacturing. Equally important are many internal activities vital to the way a company is perceived by its customers.

Customer Satisfaction

Ultimately the success of an enterprise is measured by customer satisfaction in terms of sales. Only if a company determines what the customer wants and provides products that satisfy those wants will the company be successful. Enterprise excellence requires the systematic analysis of alternative strategic opportunities for exploiting market and technical opportunities based on an understanding of the relative profitability of those strategies.

Accurate Allocation of Costs

To understand your cost structures and how to manage them well, you must know and manage your activities. A common mistake is to aggregate costs into overhead and allocate these costs without tracing them to specific products and customers. Conventional costing ignores important differences between products and services, markets, and customers, which incur different overhead costs. The broader the product line, the more distortions result from conventional costing practices. With distorted costing, some products or customers are overcharged while others are subsidized. Profitable business is lost through overpricing and unprofitable business won through underpricing.

Enterprise excellence demands information that assists managers in making decisions that result in improved product design, better product mix, and the removal of waste from operating activities. New cost management systems must support enterprise excellence by providing information on how the work is currently being performed, whether it contributes to corporate objectives, what the **drivers** of activities are, and how the system facilitates behavioral incentives to improve manufacturing effectiveness. The new cost management systems must identify how each activity in the enterprise contributes to corporate success and must encourage a commitment to total quality and continual improvement. The foundation of these new cost management systems is activity accounting.

TRADITIONAL COST SYSTEMS

In light of the revolution taking place in the business world, one would expect to see significant changes in accounting. After all, the conventional cost accounting systems were designed for a prior era when direct labor and materials were the predominant **factors of production**, technology was stable, overhead activities supported the production process, and there was a limited range of products.

In this environment, the valuation of inventory was the primary objective of cost accounting. Traditional cost accounting systems attached factory costs to products primarily to value inventory and cost of goods sold. Since the manufacturing objective was to maximize labor and machine usage, cost control was focused at the point of cost occurrence by **cost element**. Waste was generated by inefficient use of the prime factors of production.

Cost accounting techniques based on such early business conditions still prevail despite dramatic changes in manufacturing. Traditional cost accounting systems provide little information on the sources of competitive advantage. Product costs are often so inaccurate they encourage management to adopt strategies that inhibit the improvement of manufacturing. Managers are encouraged to manage the allocation and absorption of overhead rather than strive to eliminate waste and improve operational performance.

Conventional cost accounting systems assume that products and their corresponding production volume cause cost. They therefore make individual product items the focus of the cost system, and costs are classified as either direct or indirect to products. Traditional systems use production volume measures such as direct labor hours, **machine hours**, or material cost as **allocation bases** to attribute overhead costs to products.

Traditional product costing systems report a reasonably accurate product cost where overhead activity is consumed in relation to production volume. Benefits for direct employees are related to direct labor, for example, and power costs are related to machine hours.

Product costs become inaccurate, however, when overhead activities not related to production volume increase in magnitude. Enterprise activities such as engineering and field support are unrelated to current production volume. Still other activities such as purchasing, machine set-ups, and order processing are related to the number of production orders rather than production quantity. When a company allocates non–volume-related activities on volume-related bases, traditional cost accounting systems provide little insight into the relationship between the operating activities that generate the overhead cost and products. A distorted product cost results.

Traditional cost systems often encourage decisions that conflict with enterprise excellence. An overhead rate based on direct labor, for example, causes an inordinate focus on the direct labor component of cost. This happens because the costing system proclaims that direct labor is very expensive.

Where the direct labor **overhead rate** is 300 percent, for example, a manufacturing improvement will remove $1 of direct labor cost from a product that will result in an apparent saving of $3 of overhead. But the direct labor is reduced by introducing a new manufacturing process or redesigning the product, so overhead is increased by the cost of the advanced manufacturing technology and engineering activities. Thus, the direct labor reduction, in reality, increases overhead.

Another danger of direct-labor-based overhead absorption is that it encourages the attitude that the direct laborers must remain fully utilized—even if they are producing to stock—otherwise, how will overhead be absorbed?

The traditional approach to cost accounting is to break down the management of an enterprise into specialized units with rigid division of responsibility. Managers of each functional area estimate the resources, by cost category (including labor, travel, facilities, and so on), necessary to accomplish their work tasks. Managers are accountable for accomplishing their tasks with the resources assigned. An accounting system monitors, by cost element, performance for an organizational unit by comparing the cost incurred with the **budgeted** costs.

For example, a purchasing department is responsible for procuring material needed in the manufacturing process. To accomplish their function, they hire a number of buyers, secretaries, and managers. The department manager estimates the amount of travel, office supplies, office space, and other resources required to execute the department's objectives. The costs are budgeted and actual costs tracked against budget by type of resource as illustrated in the following table.

Cost Center: Procurement Department

Account	Description	Actual	Budget	Variance
0009	Wages and salaries, salaried	$ 80,150	$ 83,000	$ 2,850
0010	Wages and salaries, hourly	124,360	110,000	(14,360)
0201	Benefits, salaried	21,812	22,600	788
0202	Benefits, hourly	37,688	32,600	(5,088)
0352	Travel	62,515	70,500	7,985
0366	Facilities	32,000	32,000	0
0380	Supplies	1,394	1,500	106
0463	Training	20,240	30,000	9,760
	Total	$380,159	$382,200	$ 2,041

The assumption is that the company will be profitable if the budgeted sales are achieved and the actual cost of all departments does not exceed budgeted cost. The role of the purchasing department, in a financial sense, is to remain within budget. The practice of collecting actual cost by cost element (labor, plant and equipment, supplies, travel, and so on) facilitates comparison with budget.

Traditional cost accounting systems do not, however, provide adequate information to identify the causes of cost. In situations where costs are deemed by management to be too high, managers tend to rely on across-the-board overhead cuts to control spending in the absence of proper information. Thus, when profits decline or disappear, companies usually respond by "tightening the belt" in the wrong way at the wrong point in the enterprise. Common approaches include:

- Universal reductions in the budgets of all departments
- Freeze on wage increases
- Freeze on overhead activities
- Early retirement
- Freeze on training and nonessential travel
- Freeze on hiring
- Freeze on investments

Such well-intentioned efforts are doomed to failure; they generate a self-feeding cycle of competitive decay. They do not address the demand for overhead resources—the activities that keep people busy. There is a natural tendency for managers to cut expenditure on activities critical to the future—such as sales or marketing development and R&D—or to forgo manufacturing improvements for the short term to make profits seem better.

A viciously deteriorating cycle works itself into worsening conditions. When short-term cutbacks are removed, spending returns at least to its previous level and often to a higher level because many important activities were delayed. Deterioration in the quality of service and pressures on an overburdened staff prompt renewed spending, and overhead creeps up. The problem is that the fundamental causes of cost were not corrected.

The most common and least understood factor that touches off such a cycle is management operating with the wrong type of data—data geared to accounting rather than management. The conventional cost accounting systems present distorted, aggregated numbers based on erroneous cost behavior patterns. The information comes too late to impact decisions and does not encourage making the changes necessary to compete in the dynamic business world.

The financial information generated in traditional systems further hinders manufacturing excellence because it presents manufacturing or operating margins, not the true picture after all influenceable manufacturing, engineering, sales, and administration costs are taken into account. Finally, traditional accounting systems do not provide a clear picture of how costs and profits change as an activity volume moves up or down. Thus they are not particularly helpful to managers who must evaluate sales, marketing, or manufacturing alternatives that involve different levels of activity.

ACTIVITY ACCOUNTING

The activity accounting approach to cost management breaks down an organization into activities. An activity describes *what* an enterprise does—the way time is spent and the outputs of the process. The principal function of an activity is to convert resources (materials, labor, and technology) into outputs. Activity accounting identifies activities performed in an organization and determines their cost and performance (time and quality).

A simple and effective activity accounting system uses the following approach:

1. Determine enterprise activities.
2. Determine activity cost and performance. Performance is measured as the cost per output, time to perform the activity, and the quality of the output.
3. Determine the output of the activity. An activity measure (output) is the factor by which the cost of a process varies most directly.
4. Trace activity cost to cost objectives. Activity costs are traced to cost objectives such as products, processes, and orders based on the usage of the activity.
5. Determine corporate short-range and long-term goals (**critical success factors**). This requires an understanding of the current cost structure, which indicates how effectively operating activities deliver value to the customer.
6. Evaluate activity **effectiveness** and **efficiency**. Knowing the critical success factors (step 5) enables a company to examine what it is now doing (step 4) and the relationship of that action to achieving those goals. Everything a company does—or avoids doing—is measured against the short-and long-term goals. This provides a useful formula on which to base a decision of whether to continue performing or to restructure an activity. Also, cost control is improved by ascertaining if there are superior methods of performing an activity, identifying wasteful activities, and determining the cause of the cost.

Determining Enterprise Activities

Activity analysis identifies the significant activities of an enterprise to establish a basis for accurately describing business **operations** and determining their cost and performance. Activity analysis decomposes a large, complex organization into its elemental activities. The decomposition is accomplished by examining each organizational unit to identify its business objective and the resources allocated to achieve this objective. Activity analysis, therefore, identifies the way a company uses its resources to accomplish its business objectives.

Determining Activity Cost and Performance

The cost of an activity includes all the factors of production employed to perform an activity. The factors of production consist of people, machines, travel, supplies, computer systems, and other resources that are customarily expressed as cost elements within a **chart of accounts**. Each significant traceable factor of production is included in an activity cost.

When a cause-and-effect relationship can be established between a factor of production and a specific activity, the cost is said to be *traceable*. In many cases, tracing cost to an activity is reasonably simple because the resource is dedicated to a single activity. A purchasing clerk dedicated to the purchase order activity is an example. When a resource supports several activities, the resource usage must be split between the activities.

A purchasing department, for example, is responsible for procurement planning, vendor selection/evaluation, vendor negotiation, purchase orders, and vendor coordination. To accomplish each of these activities, the department manager will hire people, plan travel, and procure office space and other resources.

The costs are planned and tracked by activity:

Activity Description	Actual	Budget	Variance
Procurement planning	$ 29,150	$ 30,000	$ 850
Vendor selection and evaluation	43,360	45,200	1,840
Vendor negotiation	45,632	50,000	4,368
Purchase orders	121,492	120,000	(1,492)
Vendor coordination	140,525	137,000	(3,525)
Total	$380,159	$382,200	$ 2,041

How an activity manager chooses to perform an activity and the number of activity occurrences determine the resources required. For example, the activity of purchase order processing requires a person to make the purchase order decision and a computer system to perform the necessary calculations and data manipulation. Other resources, such as office supplies, are also required. The execution of these activities triggers the consumption of resources that are recorded as costs in the general ledger. The number of purchase order clerks, data-processing resources, and office supplies depends on the number of purchase orders to be processed. The cost of the activity is determined by tracing the labor, technology, and office supplies to the purchase order activity. A causal relationship is established between the factors of production and the scheduling activity.

Determining Output of the Activity

Activity cost is expressed in terms of a measure of activity volume by which the costs of a given process vary most directly (for example, number of purchase orders or number of vendors). This is known as the *activity measure*.

The activity measure is an input, output, or physical attribute of the activity. For example, the input to the purchasing activity is a purchase requisition, and the output is a purchase order. The cost of the purchasing activity can be expressed as a cost per purchase requisition or purchase order. The selection of the activity measure is critical because it makes visible the factors that drive activity volume and subsequently cost.

Tracing Activity Cost to Products, Customers, or Other Cost Objectives

Activity accounting is based on the principle that activities consume resources, whereas products, customers, or other cost objectives consume activities. Costing is enhanced by more discrete tracing of the cost of building a product, supporting a customer, or other cost objective. This is done by identifying all traceable activities and determining how much of each activity's output is dedicated to the cost objective. This cost structure, which is referred to as the *bill of activities*, describes each product's pattern of activity consumption.

The discrete tracing of cost to cost objectives, facilitated by the activity accounting system, allows a company to assess the long-term profitability of the current and future product mix. Forecasting the product mix allows the company to assess whether the current activity structure is best suited to the product mix.

The tracing of activities to users based on usage, unlike cross-subsidized allocations based on production usage overhead rates, distinguishes between intensive users and light users of an activity. Under traditional accounting, the cost associated with issuing a purchase order is allocated to products by using a basis such as direct labor, machine hours, or material cost. To properly trace costs to products requires determination of how much of each activity is consumed in a product. Consider a complex product that requires an average of 20 purchase orders while a simple product requires 1 purchase order. Accurate product cost requires that the complex product absorb a greater proportion of the purchase order activity than the simple product.

To continue the illustration, consider a procurement department that spends $120,000 processing 6,000 purchase orders. The average cost per purchase order is $20. The complex product requires $400 (20 purchase orders @ $20) of the purchase order activity, whereas the simple product requires $20 (one purchase order @ $20)—a dramatic difference.

As a result of this improved tracing process, reported product costs could vary dramatically from the traditional model. One large automotive company found that the product cost distortion was between 40 percent and 60 percent for the average component.

Determining Critical Success Factors

An important activity of top management is to develop strategic plans based on the external environment in which the business operates. Enterprise activities should be structured in line with the stated strategic plans. Line management, however, is concerned with daily operations and meeting short-term requirements. A key objective of activity accounting is to match these two perspectives.

Evaluating Activity Effectiveness and Efficiency

Managers are accountable for the continual improvement of activity performance. In structuring how an activity is performed, a business has a range of choices to make between different processing methods and resources. Each alternative method of accomplishing an activity brings with it certain implications for the business in terms of response to markets, manufacturing capabilities, the level of investment required, the unit cost, and type of control and management structure. The fundamental rationale for choosing a specific method of performing an activity is that it be best able to support the business objectives.

Activity cost is important in cost control. An *activity cost* is the ratio of resources assigned to an activity to the amount of output of the activity. An activity cost, therefore, is input divided by output—a productivity measure.

To judge the effectiveness of the purchase order activity, for example, requires knowing both the cost of the resource assigned and the number of purchase orders processed. If the cost today to process 6,000 purchase orders is $120,000, the cost per purchase order is $20. If, as the result of improvements in the purchasing department, the company is able to process 10,000 purchase orders for the same cost, the new cost per purchase order would be reduced to $12. Productivity will have been greatly improved.

ACTIVITY AND TRADITIONAL COST ACCOUNTING CONTRASTED

Activity accounting militates against the misuse of resources that usually is associated with cross-subsidized allocation. This gives activity managers an incentive to keep their operations competitive by continually identifying and cost-effectively eliminating generators of waste.

As an illustration of the differences between traditional cost accounting and activity accounting, assume a company receives a request to expedite an order. Expediting an order normally results in rescheduling (and delaying) other orders. The production costs of the rescheduled orders are increased because they involve additional material handling, increased work-in- progress costs, and additional set-up and tear-down costs.

Under traditional accounting practices, these costs would be charged as incurred to the rescheduled products and reported as an unfavorable variance by the standard cost system. Similarly, an actual cost system would report higher actual costs for the products that were rescheduled. There is no direct way of seeing that these costs were caused by the reschedule activity.

In contrast, under an activity accounting system, all events caused by the reschedule activity are linked and reported as a separate cost. The additional expediting-related activities such as set-up and tear-down are traceable to the rescheduling. This results in the elimination of the unfavorable variance for production orders affected by expediting.

This information provides valuable input back to the schedulers who caused the higher cost by making the reschedule decision. In many cases, the order might not have been rescheduled if the true costs had been known.

If a future decision to reschedule is made, then the expedited order should receive the total cost and report an unfavorable variance and lower profit margins (or loss).

It should be noted that the total department cost is the same under both the traditional (cost element) and activity accounting approaches. The difference is that under traditional cost accounting, costs are accumulated and controlled in total by cost category for each organizational unit, whereas under activity accounting, costs are associated with what the organization does (work unit).

WHY IMPLEMENT ACTIVITY ACCOUNTING?

Activity accounting has been implemented by various companies in a variety of ways to solve significantly different problems. For example, consider five pioneering companies: General Dynamics, Fort Worth Division; General Motors; Hewlett-Packard, Roseville Network Division; Martin Marietta Energy Systems; and Siemens.

General Dynamics, Fort Worth Division (GDFW)

GDFW is an aerospace and defense company that produces military aircraft.

Factors driving the need for activity accounting: GDFW felt that its existing cost accounting systems were not providing adequate information to manage the transition to the "factory of the future." The management focus of the factory modernization was on managing total factory process and functions. To be consistent with this philosophy, the cost measurement system needed to expand beyond the traditional (and myopic) direct labor cost monitoring to include the monitoring of support costs.

Objective of the activity accounting system: The objective of the activity accounting system implemented at GDFW, known as the Comprehensive Cost-Tracking System (CCTS), was to implement a cost-tracking system that could analyze the cost saving resulting from implementing factory modernization and productivity improvement programs.

The CCTS uses an activity basis for measuring cost. Activities impacted by the investment are identified. The costs of these activities, before and after implementation, are estimated. The CCTS retains the estimated costs from the cost-benefit analysis (baseline) and captures actual costs (post-implementation costs). Comparing the baseline of costs prior to the investment with the post-implementation costs quantifies the total effect of the modernization program.

General Motors

General Motors is a manufacturer of automobiles and automobile components.

Factors driving the need for activity accounting: The automobile industry was under tremendous pressure to improve competitiveness in the face of global competition.

Objective of the activity accounting system: The General Motors Activity Based Cost System (ABCS) was designed to calculate a product cost for use in **make/buy decisions**. The basis of the system was to charge direct labor and materials directly to the product and allocate **indirect costs** using a two-stage tracing procedure whereby costs are traced to activity centers and subsequently to products.

Hewlett-Packard, Roseville Network Division (HPRND)

HPRND manufactures I/O (input-output) devices for HP's computer products. These products typically consist of a printed circuit assembly.

Factors driving the need for activity accounting: The primary factors driving the need for an activity accounting system were:

- HPRND wanted to change from a product orientation to a process orientation in operations management.
- Conventional manufacturing overhead allocation provides product designers with incentives to design labor out of products but in reality overhead cost was not correspondingly reduced.

Objective of the activity accounting system: The goal of the HPRND activity accounting system was to develop a cost accounting system that better mirrors the manufacturing process. The key objectives of the system include:

- To eliminate the tracking of direct labor by assembly and product
- To control labor by activity (process)
- To control material by stock flows

The system was implemented initially for the product verification test, defect analysis/repair, mechanical assembly, and cable activities.

The significance of the HPRND activity accounting was that it followed the total quality control (TQC) methodology and defined manufacturing as a set of processes. Rather than controlling the cost of manufacturing specific products and assemblies, the focus of cost accounting was shifted to control the activities (processes) by which the product is manufactured.

So while product cost was an important output of HPRND's activity accounting system, it was a necessary but secondary output. The manufacturing environment was seen not as a single process (process accounting) or a series of production lots (job lot accounting), but as a set of processes, each of which performs a specific function. Likewise, the areas that support direct manufacturing, such as purchasing, product engineering, or scheduling, are seen as activities. Cost collection has a process rather than product focus.

Martin Marietta Energy Systems, Inc. (MMES)

MMES operates the U.S. Department of Energy (DOE) facilities in Oak Ridge, Tennessee, which produce nuclear weapons components, process special nuclear materials, and support weapon design laboratories.

Factors driving the need for activity accounting: Several factors prompted MMSE plant management to initiate efforts in 1984 to develop a more effective system for cost characterization, collection, and management. The primary ones include the following:

- *New management*. Martin Marietta was recently awarded a DOE contract to operate the Oak Ridge and Paducah facilities. With the change in management came the need to reexamine program management emphasis, including resource planning/management and accounting systems.

- *Regulated institutional activities*. Federal and state regulation of nuclear operations has increased dramatically in the areas of regulation that govern environmental protection, waste management, health and safety, radioactive contamination control, security, and nuclear materials accountability. Although MMES understood the growth in regulation-related activities in the organizations primarily responsible for their administration, their impact on operations could not be gauged with the accounting system as it existed.

- *Production support personnel*. There were minimal measures of the specific efforts and contributions of support personnel (manufacturing engineering, quality, production supervision, and so on), because this group of employees was treated strictly as production overhead.

- *Budgeting and cost management*. A system was needed to identify major cost drivers, understand their impact on the plant's operations across organizational boundaries, effectively plan the resources essential to meeting the various mission requirements (production and nonproduction), and then report performance against these resource plans in a way that would enhance management's ability to make operational decisions.

Objective of the activity accounting system: The goal of the MMES activity accounting system was to develop a better understanding of factors that cause overhead. It was believed that several general plant and overhead functions such as environmental initiatives, security, and health/safety had a significant impact on not only the responsible department but also on all organizations across the facility. Requirements in each of these functions resulted in a significant number of activities in many organizational units.

Siemens

Siemens is an electronics manufacturer. Activity accounting has been implemented at three Siemens sites: Regensburg, Bad Neustadt, and Augsburg. Each of these sites had significantly different manufacturing characteristics, as described in the following table:

	Regensburg	Bad Neustadt	Augsburg
Products	Electric in-house devices (e.g., fuses, circuit breakers)	Electric motors, low and middle sizes	Printed circuits, multilayer technique switches, and sockets
Type of production	Mass and batch	Batch and contract	Batch and contract
Annual sales (in million DM)	230	300	150
Cost structure			
Direct material	25%	43%	20%
Direct labor	9%	9%	4%
Indirect costs	66%	48%	76%
Number of products	20,000	10,000	3,000

Factors driving the need for activity accounting: The impetus for implementing activity accounting at Siemens came from two primary sources: (1) rising office support costs and (2) past successes in tracing indirect shop floor costs to products. The factory office floor cost had increased by 117 percent over the six years prior to the activity accounting system, whereas shop floor overhead increased only 34 percent. The reasons cited included increased activities associated with the development, design, customer order processing, and engineering (e.g., software production for Flexible Manufacturing System—FMS). Internal studies demonstrated that there was no cause-and-effect relationship between shop floor costs and office costs. The traditional factors of material, labor hours, and process times were not the primary factors that accounted for the increase in office support costs. A new basis of apportionment for office support activities had to be defined. Past successes in tracing indirect shop floor costs were another major motivation for developing an activity accounting system. Siemens had divided its shop floor into numerous work centers, up to 300 per plant. In addition, Siemens was a pioneer in implementing technology-accounting principles.

Objective of the activity accounting system: The activity accounting system implemented at Siemens focuses on business processes. Key business processes such as "process and store received goods" were decomposed into the requisite activities. Costs were attached to the business activities and rolled up to support product cost and cost control.

COMMON REASONS WHY COMPANIES IMPLEMENT ACTIVITY ACCOUNTING

Activity accounting is normally used to support several types of decisions. The primary ones include:

- Product cost
- Managing cash and liquidity
- Cost control
- Decision support

Product Cost

Product costs are used by managers to make pricing, estimating, make/buy, and design-to-cost decisions. A product cost is considered accurate when it mirrors the manufacturing process. The greater accuracy of product costs in an activity accounting system mitigates the problem of inappropriate messages that are conveyed by traditional systems. An inaccurate product cost increases the chances of incorrect decisions.

Accurate product cost is critical in selecting products, markets, and customers to be emphasized. Profit potential is the most important factor when assessing and selecting product and market segments. Too many companies focus on expanded sales volume with the assumption that profits will follow. However, when the fight for market share in a stable or declining market intensifies, managers must specialize in the most profitable product or service rather than increased sales volume.

Managing Cash and Liquidity

Cash and liquidity are as essential as reported profits. Cash leads to liquidity, and liquidity is critical in a business environment of high risk and great uncertainty. Cash and liquidity help withstand surprises, facilitate adaptation to sudden changes, and enable a company to capitalize on the narrow windows of opportunity that are common in a turbulent environment. A business can go bankrupt while reporting profits, but it will never go bankrupt as long as its cash and liquidity positions are strong.

The lack of concentration on cash and liquidity are apparent in most corporations. Capital expenditures are justified on projected sales volume gains or cost savings without adequate regard to the availability of funds or the cash carrying costs. Working capital is allowed to build without considering its carrying cost. Improper capital management disguises sloppy business practices. Consider work-in-progress (**WIP**) inventory. WIP hides quality and manufacturing problems by buffering their effects. These practices inevitably lead to a bloated investment base that is too large for the business base and lowers profits.

Cost Control

Cost information should encourage enterprise excellence. Waste cannot be tolerated. Products should be designed to optimize performance. Activities should support corporate objectives.

Decision Support

Cost information is used to facilitate decisions such as make/buy, pricing, and design-to-cost. Too often the managers responsible for these decisions use cost information from outside the cost management system.

Today cost information provided by the cost accounting system is not timely and is inappropriate for decision making. It is inappropriate because it is compiled on the assumption that all support activities are related to production volume and it aggregates organizational units into common cost categories. Cost data is not timely because it is generated from the monthly accounting close. Cost data should be updated to correspond to the timing of the decision—not to accounting conventions.

USING ACTIVITY ACCOUNTING FOR BEHAVIORAL CHANGE

Some companies use activity accounting as a behavioral tool to focus attention on one or two critical aspects of enterprise excellence. One company used activity accounting to focus attention on the number of parts in order to decrease engineering and materials control activities. They allocated overhead costs to products based on the number of part numbers. A positive result was that the design engineers designed new products with fewer components.

This company used the number of part numbers as an activity measure for procurement, storage, receiving, and part database maintenance activities. Because each part number received the same cost regardless of production volume, the cost per part was much less for high-volume part numbers than for low-volume part numbers. This made it more expensive for the product designer to use a low-volume unique component than a high-volume common component. The choice of output measures was behaviorally consistent with the firm's manufacturing strategy.

Design engineers used substantially fewer unique components in their product designs. In three years, the part count for the division fell to one-fourth its previous level while the number of vendors fell to less than one-seventh in the same time period. Procurement overhead fell, quality improved, and several products that had previously been produced on separate lines were produced on the same line.

However, this accounting practice distorted product cost. Many costs do not vary on the number of part numbers. The resulting cost distortions decrease the relevance of product cost in decisions that depend on an accurate product cost. To use the number of part numbers as an activity measure, we must be aware that it bypasses the following cause-and-effect chain:

- The cost of the purchasing activity is related to the number of suppliers and the number of purchase orders.

- The activity measure is the number of purchase orders, or purchase order lines, because purchasing resources vary by this factor.
- The cost drivers are the primary factors driving the need for the purchasing activity, and cost avoidance is achieved by managing these drivers. The key cost drivers include the make/buy strategy, the number of production orders, and the number of components in the product. However, to use these as activity measures requires successive approximations that lead to a very inaccurate tracing of cost to products.

The selection of an activity measure might result in changes in organizational behavior that does not match with strategic goals. For instance, people may modify their performance in a way that lowers their cost per activity but may increase inventory.

HOW ACTIVITY ACCOUNTING HELPS ACHIEVE ENTERPRISE EXCELLENCE

Activity accounting provides a foundation for achieving enterprise excellence by eliminating distortions and cross-subsidization caused by traditional **cost allocations**, and it provides a base line for improving cost and performance. Activity cost information provides a clear view of how the mix of a company's diverse products, services, and activities contributes in the long run to the bottom line. Cost reduction potential is made visible through non–value added analysis and best practices.

Nonfinancial information, to control operating activities, and activity cost information when combined provide the management information that businesses need in today's competitive environment. Activity information is the key to continual improvement of profitability.

Activity accounting helps a company achieve enterprise excellence by:

- Improving make/buy, estimating, and pricing decisions that are based on a product cost that mirrors the manufacturing process
- Facilitating elimination of waste by providing visibility of non–value added activities
- Identifying the source of cost by identifying the cost drivers
- Linking corporate strategy to operational decision making, thus enabling management to capitalize on activities that are a corporate strength while restructuring activities that do not contribute to achieving corporate objectives

- Providing **feedback** on whether the anticipated results of the strategies are obtained so that corrective action can be initiated
- Ensuring that time, quality, flexibility, and conformance to schedule goals are achieved by linking performance measures to strategy
- Encouraging continual improvement and total quality control because planning and control are directed at the process level
- Improving the effectiveness of budgeting by identifying the cost/performance relationship of different service levels
- Improving profitability by monitoring total **life-cycle cost** and performance
- Providing insight into the fastest-growing and least visible element of cost—overhead
- Ensuring achievement of investment plans by monitoring the investment through the activity accounting system so that when deviations from plan are detected, corrective action can be initiated
- Continually evaluating the effectiveness of activities to identify potential investment opportunities
- Incorporating externally set target performance and cost goals and setting of specific goals at the activity level
- Eliminating many crises by fixing the problems rather than treating symptoms

It is also important to stress that the cost management system will do nothing but identify where potential problems are encountered. It is what people do with the information that will determine whether cost management is a success.

GETTING STARTED

Before starting an activity analysis, it is important to consider that the effort involved in gathering, analyzing, and recording information on activities demands time, money, and manpower; it is not an effort that should be undertaken lightly or without considerable forethought. Ask yourself these questions:

- Does top management understand the value and effort of implementing an activity accounting system? Are top managers willing to commit the required time, money, and resources?

• Do managers and supervisors understand the changes that may be recommended as a result of the activity accounting system? Do they realize how such changes might affect them and their employees?

SUMMARY

Activity accounting reshapes the way companies manage costs. It attaches company costs to activities. Product cost is the sum of the cost of all *traceable* activities based on the usage of the activity. Cost control is focused on the source of the cost regardless of the organizational unit in which it is incurred.

Managers need activity information to help them achieve enterprise excellence. Activity accounting identifies what the organizaton does. In order to improve profitability and performance, it is critical to understand where the enterprise's precious time goes and, in detail, what the enterprise does and how it does it. Ultimately, an organization can only improve when management understands what is done, how well it is done, and whether it contributes to corporate objectives. Activity accounting facilitates improved traceability and, ultimately, improved accountability.

Activity accounting is a powerful tool for managing the complex operations of a business through a detailed assessment of its activities. Activity accounting attributes cost and performance data to activities. Activity cost and performance data provide management with information needed to determine an accurate product cost, improve business processes, eliminate waste (non–value added activities), identify cost drivers, plan operations, and set business strategies.

Activity accounting generates cost and production information in a manner that drives continual improvement and total quality. Continual improvement and total quality control are facilitated by treating each activity as a process and identifying the *source* of cost rather than focusing on the *symptoms*. In focusing attention on the source of problems, management must assign responsibility to those departmental activities that drive cost and monitor their execution to see if the planned results were achieved.

Activity information allows managers to identify and eliminate waste. It also confirms progress in removing waste from operating activities.

Eliminating waste and implementing a philosophy of continual improvement is not difficult if senior management has the will and if the cost management system is set up to assist. They can be impossible, however, if the accounting systems are designed around functional organizations rather than around activities.

2

THE CHANGING
BUSINESS ENVIRONMENT

The purpose of this chapter is to:

- Describe the changes in the business environment that lead to the development of activity accounting
- Project future manufacturing trends and their impact on management reporting

The business environment is awash with change. Until recently, such staples of today's business life as the personal computer and the fax did not exist; manufacturing companies used inventory to buffer against uncertainty; robots were found only in horror stories; South Korea was still considered a cheap-labor Third World country; and free enterprise was still a forbidden notion within the Communist bloc.

Now, quite suddenly, these disparate changes are coming together in a cascade that is causing massive reappraisals of basic business assumptions and expectations that have long remained unquestioned. The current wave of technological and management transformation coupled with global competition is altering the attitudes and expectations of companies around the world and, in the process, creating new markets and business organizations.

The new business organizations face the formidable task of simultaneously improving quality and customer service and reducing cost. To remain competitive, firms must streamline **operations**, eliminate waste, adopt a commitment to total quality, and judiciously incorporate advanced technologies such as just-in-time, robotics, computer-aided design, and flexible manufacturing systems into their facilities. Manufacturing is a competitive weapon that changes the basis of competition through new product capabilities and manufacturing excellence. Global competition has forced companies to adopt new manufacturing technology and philosophies or risk loss of market share.

The dilemma facing most companies is that their facilities, management, and systems were developed for a different business environment. The resulting manufacturing and management practices are a hodgepodge of the traditional and the progressive. The software and hardware are in place, the procedures are understood, the people who receive information from the system know how to interpret it. The system is "frozen" in the sense that people are comfortable with its use. The bottom line is that change is difficult yet management inertia is paralyzing.

Amid such profound and rapid change, the principles by which we have been accustomed to managing companies and the tools we have used to measure progress have become obsolete. Time-honored cost accounting systems present a distorted view of the enterprise and do not provide the visibility necessary to encourage a commitment to continuous improvement and total quality.

Managers seeking to succeed in this environment are turning to their **management accounting** system for new types of information. Improved **capital budgeting** techniques, more accurate product cost data, and more relevant performance evaluation information are needed. Today the crucial link between manufacturing excellence and measurement systems is being rediscovered.

THE DECLINE OF TRADITIONAL MANUFACTURING

Traditional manufacturing companies have taken a beating during the last few years. These companies were organized along functional lines. Based on the premise that repetition, experience, and homogeneity of tasks promote efficiency, functional manufacturing clusters (like machines and processes at the same location within a factory) developed with movement of work-in-progress inventory between them as the product is manufactured.

In this system low cost is achieved through economies of scale and high quality through constant inspection and detection of defective parts. Direct labor is considered the dominant factor of production, and the role of technology (plant, equipment, and information systems) is to increase the productivity of the direct laborer. John Kenneth Galbraith proudly proclaimed that the production problem was solved.

Functional manufacturing created specialized laborers. It was believed that highly trained specialists, who were fully utilized, minimized cost. The result was that the boom years of the 1960s created an environment where workers demanded higher wages and lenient working conditions. Management and labor unions were enemies. With skilled labor in short supply and product requirements tightening, managers could never quite bring themselves to say "no."

Functional manufacturing was linked to the economic order quantity (EOQ) model. The EOQ model, unchallenged by Western manufacturing companies, represented the optimum (least-cost) production lot size. Under EOQ, the cost of holding inventories—the cost of capital, storage, insurance, depreciation—was balanced against the cost of production start-up—the cost of placing orders, set-up, shipping, material movement, quantity discounts lost—to derive the optimum order quantity. According to the EOQ model, the setup cost per unit goes down as the batch size increases; consequently, a firm should produce in larger batches to incur the setup cost less frequently.

Functional manufacturing and the EOQ model required exorbitant levels of inventory to buffer against uncertainty and ensure high efficiency by keeping all factors of production fully utilized. It was not unusual to have 10 to 15 changeovers a day, resulting in costly **work centers** being idle far too long while the fully utilized operator switched products. The manufacturing plant that evolved became characterized by one term: redundancy. Multiple machines, requiring multiple time-consuming set-ups and buffered by large inventories, were used to decouple the manufacturing process from demand, while management sought ways to capitalize on economies of scale.

The result was an unresponsive manufacturing plant characterized by long **lead times**, significant quality problems, and complex forecasting techniques. Lead times were protracted because **cycle time** was secondary to resource utilization. It was not unusual for queue times awaiting processing to account for 95 percent of the total production cycle time. Frequent changeovers often created quality problems or amplified existing ones.

The long production cycles resulted in an increased dependence on forecasts. The problem became circular. Basing production on forecasts, which are uncertain by nature, caused considerable reordering of priorities and other disruptions to the manufacturing process. The result, more often than not, was confusion and inefficiency on all levels; inventories of the wrong items grew while the number of back orders led to manufacturing inefficiency and infighting between marketing and production. This, in turn, increased cycle time.

The manufacturing complexity inherent in functional manufacturing gave rise to the need for mathematical programming and complex production and control systems. Given long lead times, significant set-ups, elaborate organizations, and instability, it was believed that competitive advantage could be achieved through optimization of resource usage. Thus emerged MRP. MRP was highly touted as an important tool to deal with long lead times—both in raw materials and in production—and constant demand fluctuation. Western manufacturers spent millions of dollars to install MRP systems, often with minimal benefit.

In this environment, computer information systems proliferated. The resources required to create and maintain the computer applications grew exponentially. Yet the credibility of the data processing department was not high. Users accepted the fact that systems development would cost more and take longer than promised. Each function demanded support from the centralized data processing staff that promised the changes when the schedule permitted.

Worse still, the customers weren't satisfied. The marketplace demanded a continual stream of new products. And every new product had markedly higher performance demands. With each new product came increased quality and reliability demands, along with shorter delivery schedules and increasing price competition.

Managers were fixated on direct labor because it represented a large proportion of total cost. They assumed that improvements in productivity came primarily from lower labor costs. As a result, companies turned manufacturing over to developing countries with large and cheap labor pools.

Conventional cost accounting systems exacerbated the problems. These systems viewed responsibility reporting as synonymous with control of **direct costs**. Thus cost measurement focused on labor efficiencies, purchase price variances, overhead allocation, and maximization of profit through control of variable costs. Proper control of direct costs required an army of cost accountants dedicated to tracking costs incurred in the shop. This legion of accountants could tell management the direct labor and material component of product cost down to the fifth decimal place.

Management information was not timely. Monthly reports would indicate that certain production orders gobbled inordinate amounts of resources, but these reports arrived at the plant weeks after the orders were complete. The line people would then try to reconstruct the previous month's or day's events to explain to management what led to the disappointing variances.

The late-arriving corporate reports, exclusively containing financial and accounting data, were of little help for operational decision making. The data were simply too aggregated and too old. Meanwhile, the plant maintained many private, manual records, a practice that was both expensive and time-consuming. As a result, the plant people relied mainly on hunches to make critical business decisions.

Reports for regulatory agencies, weekly production reports for corporate headquarters, and so forth, consumed an increasing amount of data processing resources. Manual gathering of more data was prohibitively expensive.

Inflation encouraged inefficiency and complacency. As long as companies could pass on inefficiencies to the customers in higher prices, there was limited incentive to tighten the belt. Complacency was heightened by an attitude that the marketplace had no choice but to accept price increases.

Meanwhile, during the late 1970s Japan was changing the basis of competition in the world market, thus signalling the end of the era of complacency and the beginning of price erosion. As a first step, several Japanese firms combined large-scale production with focused factories to achieve an economic advantage through high-volume, low-variety production. In particular, the automobile, construction equipment, and consumer electronics industries faced ruthless competition from Japan and the emerging Pacific Rim nations. Prices had to be reduced every year to maintain market share in these critical industries. The result was bankruptcy for many companies and a squeeze on profit margins for those that remained.

It appeared to Western managers obsessed with direct labor that the Japanese manufacturers were **dumping** their products on the world market. In most cases companies did not understand how the Japanese could produce a higher-quality product at lower cost.

Other significant events were transforming manufacturing. While attention in Western companies was centered on direct labor and Japanese dumping, Toyota was quietly developing a new type of production system that combined the economies of large-scale production with the advantage of product variety. This marked the emergence of just-in-time manufacturing.

Many companies were not to survive this transition period: companies that had seen little or no profit. Several quarters in a row had produced nothing but red ink. "Dividend" was a foreign word to the stockholders. With each quality reject came a muddled promise that "we won't let it happen again." Missed contracts elicited an optimistic "we'll do it better next time."

Management responded with across-the-board cost reductions. Senior executives announced that many plants were "an endangered species." Unions reacted by calling urgent meetings during which the workers on the shop floor were asked to take the first (and, not surprisingly, the largest) cuts. The unions realized that a plant closing in a region already experiencing high unemployment would be devastating and agreed to the cuts. Overtime was abolished. This was followed by layoffs.

Even the administrative offices were affected: Yes, it was announced that there would be a mandatory cut in office supplies and white collar employees would now be expected to pay for their own coffee.

For a while things looked promising. Companies exploited hidden reserves and manipulated accounting policies to report steady earnings and continue their happy talk. Self-satisfied top managers declared, "The program is on track!" They were almost ready to reinstate their bonus plans, blindly ignoring the structural weaknesses. They were like the sailor on the Titanic who told a newspaperman, "Mister, God Almighty couldn't sink this ship."

Then companies ran out of fat to trim. The grim reality of aging plant equipment; a frustrated, embittered, and underproductive work force; and no vision for the future came crashing in. During the 1970s and 1980s the stockholders in many companies overwhelmingly approved takeovers that management had argued were "unfriendly." This time, the layoffs came at the top.

HARD AUTOMATION HITS THE SHOP FLOOR

The new managers seemed to know what they were doing. Rather than retrench further, they stated that they wanted to "revitalize the company from the shop floor up." Technology promised an opportunity to recapture a competitive edge. The initial focus of the capital investment strategy was on replacing obsolete processes. After they had rebuilt their factories, they would begin to use technology as a competitive weapon. The new managers had visions of a highly automated plant—a plant that would change the basis of competition in the marketplace. Wickham Skinner's message that a manufacturing facility can be either a competitive weapon or a corporate millstone was to become a stark reality.

Managers were caught up in the whirlwind of technology. They watched as Lee Iacocca rebuilt Chrysler. Then they began to act. First several old machines were replaced with numerically controlled milling machines. Next automated storage and retrieval systems (AS/RS) were installed in the main stockrooms. Then complete flexible machining systems (FMSs) were prototyped for use on new high-performance components under research and development. In addition to an advanced machining center, the FMS included an automated material feeder, a robotic parts manipulator, and an automated tool changer. Sensor-based adaptive inspection was part of the machining process. Companies began to win production contracts, and their FMSs became full-scale production work cells installed on the shop floor. Before long, several new work cells dotted shop floors. Companies proudly proclaimed to the business world that they were committed to multimillion-dollar capital investment programs.

The new technologies created new management challenges. The accelerating rate of technological change multiplied the number of new products. The R&D department was brimming with new products and expanded features amid new materials. The marketing department agreed that new products were critical to the future. As these products replaced the current product line, manufacturing capabilities had to be upgraded.

One such revolutionary manufacturing technology confronted by the electronics industry was surface mount technology (SMT)—a process of mounting devices (integrated circuits and the like) onto printed circuit boards (PCBs). SMT superceded through-hole mounting of devices in printed circuit boards. Surface mount increased board capacity by a factor of two. This meant better and faster products—qualitatively and quantitatively. SMT required an entirely different set of manufacturing processes that were capital-intensive in contrast to the labor-intensive through-hole insertion process.

Surface mount technology meant a new generation of products. It was estimated that by the early 1990s half of the production of printed circuit boards was to be with SMT. However, R&D departments projected that by early in the next century SMT was to be an obsolete technology. Through-hole technology enjoyed essentially a 30-year life cycle, while SMT's life cycle was forecasted to last approximately 15 years.

An important reason R&D departments projected a short life cycle for SMT is that the follow-on technology was already under development: three-dimensional (or silicon-on-silicon) ICs (integrated circuits). Three-dimensional ICs were to do away with PCBs altogether. This would completely restructure the electronics industry. Other industries faced similar technology challenges.

The short life cycles along with the proliferation of products put pressure on the design engineer to bring products to the market much more quickly, to get the design right before it went into production, and to streamline the product abandonment process.

It often took a company one to three years to introduce a new product. Management recognized that the product introduction process had to be streamlined by more tightly coupling activities to eliminate wasted time. Gone was the old practice of redesigning the product and its manufacturing processes after it had been released to manufacturing. There was simply not enough time to recover the waste generated by an ineffective product introduction process.

"Design for manufacturability" became a key banner. A company product life-cycle study revealed that by the time 5 percent of the **product development** budget had been spent, more than 80 percent of the final product cost was locked in by decisions made by marketing, R&D, and the engineering departments.

The study pointed out that the product design and manufacturing processes selected were a function of product performance requirements, physical properties of the materials involved, and manufacturing capabilities and limitations of the facility. The product specifications locked in the majority of the material cost because the performance characteristics and product cost goals were normally delineated at this time. The selection of material was, in turn, a primary determinant of the alternative manufacturing processes.

Thus product design and manufacturing process decisions were the most important determinants of a company's cost structure. The study concluded that the current engineering design emphasis was on product features, leaving many of the decisions on selection of equipment to be made on an ad hoc basis by manufacturing and operational personnel.

Shorter product life cycles resulted in less latitude for management error, since they involved shorter cost recovery periods. Managers realized that they would have to spend considerably more money and time in planning activities to lower production costs, reduce time from design to manufacture, improve quality, increase flexibility, and lower product life-cycle costs.

As a consequence, management made a significant commitment to modernize engineering. In many companies, drafting was automated using computer-aided design (CAD) workstations. Additional computers were installed to automate computer-aided engineering (CAE) activities such as finite element modeling. Engineering overhead began to creep up as the emphasis to design and manufacture the product with fewer iterations required additional engineering resources.

The number of new products increased dramatically because many companies believed that a full range of products would attract customers. While the number of new products was on the increase, however, very few products were abandoned. Marketing departments cited customer expectations as a reason for keeping outdated products. Thus the number of components proliferated, and companies produced many small batches of parts. The constant flow of new products, when coupled with decreasing product life cycles, meant that plant management couldn't be sure what the product mix would be in three to four years. The implication, therefore, was clear: Flexibility at every level of operation was mandatory.

A similar phenomenon was shortening the manufacturing plant and equipment life cycles. Much of the new manufacturing equipment used computer technology, in which significant advances occur at very frequent intervals—generally every three years or less. Technological obsolescence replaced physical obsolescence as the primary determinant for machine replacement.

Automation and flexibility were often at odds. Automation led to a higher percentage of fixed cost because of its capital intensity. The old labor-intensive manufacturing environment had enabled management to cut costs during a recession by laying off workers, a luxury not available when managing robots and numerically controlled manufacturing systems.

The changes extended well beyond the factory floor. Personal computers (PCs) were introduced to help streamline the work load of the office worker. Typewriters were replaced by word processors and word-processing applications on PCs. PCs running electronic spreadsheets seemed to sprout up everywhere.

With the introduction of advanced manufacturing technologies came an increased dependence on computerized information. The manufacturing requirements planning (MRP) system was expanded to a full manufacturing resources planning (MRPII) system. The mainframe computer configuration was expanded correspondingly.

Management intuitively believed that the complete, accessible data provided by the MRPII system could provide a much better insight into the increasingly complex manufacturing process. However, management did not have a mechanism for evaluating the cost effects of more accurate information, data validation, or poor decisions based on incorrect data. Additionally, many of the information flows that were originally manual had to be integrated to ensure that information was timely and accurate. Much of the information that was processed in batch mode now had to be processed in real time.

The role of the laborer changed dramatically. Prior to the computer, knowledge resided with humans. The objective of manufacturing technology was to increase worker productivity. With automation the skills and composition of the shop floor worker began to change. Companies that introduced advanced manufacturing technologies found that much of the manufacturing knowledge was transferred from the operator to the programmer who created the machine instructions. No longer must the person running an NC lathe be a skilled machinist, nor must the manufacturing process be synchronized with the laborer. The technology controlled the pace of manufacturing; the laborer assisted and monitored. The workers remaining on the shop floor tended increasingly to become highly skilled computer technicians.

A similar change was occurring in the labor-management relationship. To compete, workers and managers were forced to recognize that industry could no longer be an arena of class warfare if companies were to match their overseas rivals.

By the late 1980s most of the technology acquired during the previous years was operational. The impact of automation on direct labor was significant. Automation, either directly or indirectly, reduced direct touch labor through the substitution of improved processes or procedures. It was not uncommon for direct touch labor to account for only 8 to 12 percent of total cost at many factories. However, the reduction in direct labor was not free. Overhead costs rose dramatically and far exceeded direct labor costs in many industries.

The survivors were leaner and fitter, well placed to expand when the economy rebounded. Manufacturing output climbed, yet the goods were being produced by fewer workers. The automobile industry was a striking example of just how much business had been transformed. Cooperation replaced conflict on the shop floor, and productivity soared. During the 1980s car production in the United Kingdom jumped more than 40 percent while direct labor was trimmed by a third, mainly through retirement.

However, in many cases automation did not provide a very potent strategic weapon because manufacturers often automated the wrong things or cost reductions simply matched similar improvements by competitors. The manufacturing process itself was inefficient and outmoded, and the competitive position was not improved merely by automation. Managers discovered that they did not possess a monopoly on advanced manufacturing technologies. Competitors who implemented strategically important technologies gained a competitive advantage through reduced cost, improved quality, faster **throughput** time, and better response to customers. There were still schedule slippages. Many management and support personnel spent the greater part of the working day attending meetings, discussing status, or chasing parts and paper throughout the enterprise. Even the engineers were spending more time fixing problems through engineering change notices than actually designing.

As a result, much of the market continued to be lost to cheaper, better-quality foreign competition. In particular, competition was significant for products with large production volumes. Through a joint **strategic planning** effort involving marketing, accounting, engineering, and manufacturing, many companies abandoned the high-volume product market and concentrated on the customized product market niche. Through hard work these companies managed to hold onto this area of the market but with small profit margins. Companies became alarmed by high overhead rates. There was no argument that the companies' indirect costs were a formidable—and expanding—component of the overall cost structure. Ironically, the same shop floor modernization efforts that resulted in steep direct labor cost reductions had contributed to indirect cost increases. The capital cost of all that new equipment hit the cost ledgers as depreciation expense. Programming costs increased as did the technical support and maintenance costs for the new, more complex machinery.

However, the increasing overhead was not due exclusively to automation. The number of personnel classified as white-collar nontouch labor ballooned. And top management pronounced: "We're too top-heavy"; "Try looking above the shop floor"; or "We can't afford all those paper-pushers." The reason for the expansion in white-collar jobs was nebulous. External paperwork increased, internal paperwork increased, and more people were brought in to keep up with the ever-expanding work load. In fact, some of the hourly employees whose jobs were eliminated by automation on the shop floor never really left the company at all. They just transferred into the ranks of the myriad indirect employees who supported engineering and operations.

With automation came a significant amount of debt—advanced technologies were not cheap. As long as the technologies contributed a positive cash flow, the resulting savings would offset the debt expense. However, inappropriate investments are catastrophic and simply mortgage the future. Not only must future products be profitable, but they must also support the cost of past investment blunders. Many companies relied on a traditional product costing system that distributed indirect costs to products with direct labor hours. Management knew that as overhead increased dramatically, the direct labor allocations distorted product cost. In the early 1980s the product costing system was redesigned using machine hours.

As quarter after quarter of financial results were reported, the promises of improved performance were not realized. Management anxiously waited for the company profits to improve dramatically, as promised by the advocates of technology. The painted factory floor glistened, and the productivity gap was narrowed dramatically. Yet profits remained marginal.

In hindsight, the reason is woefully apparent—a frightening inability of top management to recognize the emerging changes. The islands of automation employed advanced manufacturing technologies to increase the productivity of the individual manufacturing process without attacking the real "cancer"— waste. Manufacturing was in a period of transition, and solutions such as the focused factory and islands of automation were simply a continuation of traditional practices.

Automation was an illusory prelude to a new manufacturing environment, an era that would not be understood until a few years later. The continued deterioration of manufacturing was a result of outdated philosophies.

Management needed to look no further than its competition for the answer. The productivity improvements were necessary merely to remain in business. They came largely from workers and managers adjusting to the economic realities and reversing decades of decline.

What Western management failed to recognize was that the most effective way to increase productivity was to eliminate problems rather than treat symptoms. MRP was one example of this conceptual failure. Rather than minimize product diversity and long lead times, companies spent millions of dollars and countless management hours implementing a system to schedule materials. Companies attempted to develop a sophisticated scheduling system rather than treat the fundamental problems.

The tidal wave that had begun in Japan began to be felt in the West. The complaints about dumping began to quiet down as study teams made pilgrimages to Japan and returned from the promised land with panaceas such as JIT, quality circles, kanban, and total quality management (TQM). If only Western companies could swallow this medicine, they could compete on the world market. Progressive companies that implemented these concepts reported glowing results.

JIT production embodies simplification and elimination of waste on the plant floor by cutting cycle time and eliminating mistakes. It is characterized by cellular manufacturing supported by vendor management and logistics improvements to minimize queue and move time and, consequently, inventories. JIT/TQM involves substantial reductions in set up times and a streamlining of the factory layout and material control to allow batch sizes to be reduced.

Companies that installed JIT found that the new system made supplier relations extremely important. Instead of the traditional adversarial relationship between supplier and customer, companies developed hand-in-hand working relationships with their suppliers. Quality problems, particularly between suppliers and users, became important.

Inventory and space needs were reduced, and, most important, production time was dramatically compressed. The production process was faster and the cash flow quicker. As lead time and flow time were reduced, forecasting became more accurate. Lead times were reduced to one day for many parts, enabling the material planners to forecast only for tomorrow rather than for the next several weeks. Over time a very effective synchronous-flow production system emerged.

Quality levels improved, due partly to the new equipment but also to the use of quality circles, statistical process control (SPC), and a new commitment on the part of shop floor workers. Just as important was the time spent afterward drinking beer and chatting. Social prejudices and suspicions began to fade after these face-to-face contacts. The result was expanded worker involvement to discover and correct problems—rather than to bury them until luck ran out and then merely rework the rejected parts. Companies moved away from confrontation toward dialogue.

As companies embraced the new manufacturing philosophies, the rules of competition were changed to include the simultaneous achievement of flexibility, quality, and low cost. In many industries the changes did not increase profitability but were a matter of survival. Companies either adopted the new manufacturing philosophies or went out of business.

Companies have now begun to reconsider their roles in the international market. New technologies of worldwide communications and transportation have redrawn the economic playing field. European industries no longer compete against Japanese or American industries. Rather, a company with headquarters in Italy, production facilities in Taiwan, and a marketing force spread throughout the world competes with other similarly global companies.

With the rise of the global corporation, managers, shareholders, and employees span the world. A company's success creates a big billboard that says, "This market exists and here is how to exploit it." The old protectionist strategy of fending off global competition gives way to a strategy of using worldwide operations to provide a buffer against currency valuation changes and to expand markets. A foreign presence increases sales and gives companies access to new technology and marketing ideas. The experience helps them fend off competition at home from foreign rivals that have jumped into the local markets. And when the economy slows, a company can reduce the risk of an economic downturn by looking to faster-growing overseas markets.

Globalization has caused as many dramatic changes in the role of the worker as has technology. In the 1980s the real earnings of the unskilled workers declined while the real wages of the knowledge worker increased.

More and more the competitiveness of a worker depends not only on the individual country's economic health but on the worker's function within the global economy. Simply stated, a global economy will not pay for non–value added activities. Workers who perform unnecessary and wasteful activities will not fit into the global economy because once competition has eliminated these activities, the remaining companies must trim them or face the loss of market share. This change has given rise to a growing number of impoverished workers and a widening gap between the rich and the poor.

Another impact of globalization is that workers who perform routine services involving tasks that are repeated over and over must settle for low wages in order to hold onto their jobs. Although we often associate these jobs with the manufacturing process, they are common among many support workers who spend their days processing data, often putting information into computers or taking it out within large centralized facilities. They are overseen by supervisors who, in turn, are monitored by more supervisors. With relative ease corporations can relocate the production facilities to take advantage of lower wages in other parts of the world. The global economy places limits on how much it will pay for these activities. Through satellite communications even routine clerical work can be undertaken far from the central offices.

Cost accounting systems became increasingly irrelevant as radical changes swept most companies. Their continued use hindered manufacturing excellence by encouraging inappropriate business decisions. Consider, for instance, that labor efficiency and machine utilization measurements motivate a supervisor to keep employees busy regardless of whether the product is built to inventory rather than demand; or that purchase price variance motivates the purchasing agent to buy in large volumes to achieve quantity discounts even though there is a significant cost to holding inventory; or that the emphasis on direct labor encourages manufacturing managers to try to achieve productivity improvements primarily by using machines more efficiently—while overhead costs soar.

In the late 1980s company management heard about a new method of costing called activity accounting. The aim of the new system was complete traceability of all factors that impact cost and performance. Armed with this information a company could more effectively make changes. Management wanted information faster so it could respond more quickly.

The difference between the product cost reported under the traditional and activity accounting systems was dramatic. The activity accounting system revealed that a high percentage of the company's products generated losses in the long run. In general, many products identified as profitable by the traditional product costing system were found to be unprofitable by the activity accounting system. In many cases a company's disappointing performance was a direct consequence of distorted cost information that contributed to management decisions to fill its line with unprofitable products.

The product cost was higher than reported for some products and lower for others. The ramifications of such miscosting were tremendous because it resulted in cross-subsidization of products. Products that were overcosted attracted competition that undercut the price. Products that were undercosted faced negligible competition. As a result, market share simultaneously increased for the undercosted products and decreased for the overcosted products. Profit therefore decreased at a greater percentage since overcosted products were subsidizing undercosted ones.

Companies were led to believe—incorrectly—that they possessed a strategic advantage in the niche markets and were at a competitive disadvantage in markets with repetitive products. They then began to restructure their manufacturing facilities based on the miscosting phenomenon. Thus it became a self- fulfilling prophecy.

A VISION OF THE FUTURE

It is practically impossible to predict exactly what the business world will be like in 10 years and how it will function. One thing is sure, however; it will be radically different from the one that currently prevails, and the transition from the business of today to that of the future will continue to be characterized by major discontinuities.

These discontinuities are important to managers for two fundamental reasons: (1) Manufacturing practices to cope with changes in the market and the competitive environment will be different and surprising, and (2) there is no assurance that business organizations that have been successful in the past will continue to prosper during and after this transition. Taken together, these developments constitute a wave of change that challenges the existing policy of most companies. To successfully confront the future, companies must reconsider the very foundations of their existing enterprise. Business has, however, undergone major transitions in the past, and some of history's lessons remain relevant today. Thus companies look to the future not so much to predict it as to systematically remind themselves how different it will be from the recent past.

The potential economic impact of emerging producers, such as India, China, and Brazil, on today's leading producers will transform the economic landscape. In 1992 the dismantling of internal common market barriers will add to the competitiveness in Europe. The introduction of "iron curtain" products to the free world together with the opening of these markets to the West will again rearrange established patterns.

Technological advancement will undoubtedly continue at an accelerating pace. It is imperative, therefore, for management to develop a vision of the future and to boldly make the changes necessary to execute the plan. A key to success is the capability of an organization to create a vision of the future *and* manage the achievement of the vision. Too often top managers do not take decisive action until it is too late because they believe that to identify problems would largely be to identify their own failings. As a result, caution becomes paralyzing.

Over the next years we will see the development of:

- "Designer materials"
- Neural/optical computers
- Holography
- Biotechnology
- Computer/human interfunctional enterprise

These technologies will reverberate throughout our global societies and profoundly impact the way we currently conceive, design, engineer, and manufacture products. The profound impacts will come when these technologies "rub up" against one another, when a breakthrough in one area will ripple through to another, adding capability. We now live in a much less linear world.

These changes will force companies in advanced nations to compete with three resources: capital, technology, and knowledge. Knowledge is found in large pools of educated professionals exposed to innovative, world-class methods, tools, and systems. The central offices of the global business will be filled with knowledge workers who manipulate information and then export their knowledge around the world. A company won't export its products; instead, it will manufacturer them in factories all over the globe. The headquarters will export strategic planning and related management services.

Elimination of waste will be a hallmark of the successful company. Work-in-progress inventory will not be tolerated. Activities originating from error corrections will be scrutinized. Unnecessary paperwork will be purged. The challenge is to perform all activities correctly the first time. This requires getting the workers involved directly in fixing the cause of the problem through programs such as just-in-time and total quality management.

The future will be characterized by a movement toward flexibility and responsiveness. The 1990s will showcase flexible machine centers that allow firms to increase responsiveness to customer demands and thereby reap the advantages of economies of scope (such as variety). As it becomes feasible to reduce lot sizes to one, rescheduling practically disappears, lead time goes to zero, and hourly shop floor planning becomes possible. Flexible manufacturing, when coupled with the concept of JIT, eliminates inventory buffer. This combination of reduced inventory and fewer, more flexible machines translates to a drastic decline in space requirements. The total picture is one of leanness: one machine for several products/processes, wasting no resources in non–value adding set-ups and yielding competitive advantages through both enhanced responsiveness and reduced costs.

The market will demand customized products with short introduction cycles. The streamlining of business processes is crucial to getting products to the market in a timely fashion.

A key element of the new manufacturing environment is time compression. The production process becomes the buffer between a dynamic market and the manufacturer. Time compression is a central element in the focused factory, JIT production, and CIM manufacturing strategies. All functions in the organization from product development to manufacturing to logistics support must be restructured to reduce time. The benefits of a flexible manufacturing system, for example, would be offset if the firm does not reduce the time it takes to process manufacturing orders. Often the key to time compression is as basic as simplifying the approval process.

The shift in costs from labor to technology is complete in a CIM environment, as many indirect labor functions such as order entry are automated. Computer-integrated manufacturing (CIM) provides an automatic link among the seemingly diverse threads of the manufacturing enterprise, including product design, manufacturing engineering, the factory floor, and logistics. With CIM, previously separate groups work in unison to achieve corporate goals. For example, product introduction cycles are decreased through the use of a common database to design the part and automatically specify the tools and fixtures needed to manufacture the part, its bill of materials, and the process plan for its manufacture. CIM links the various islands of automation into one integrated system that seeks to optimize the performance of an entire enterprise.

Accelerating technological innovation will increasingly rely on information and communication technologies. The future system will be software-dependent. The task of processing and controlling information in the factory of the future will require reconceptualization of the role of data processing and the use of new techniques such as object-oriented systems, which allow the application programming to be shifted to the users of the data.

Information and communications requirements and capabilities will be more than double what they are now. The potential will be there by the opening of the twenty-first century to have the enterprise totally integrated from the supplier to the customer. The impact on manufacturing will be to transfer routine knowledge from humans to computer systems.

As companies' production facilities evolve into factories of the future, common shared data are critical. The data used by different organizations often overlap by 80 to 90 percent. Efficiency dictates that no data should ever be entered more than once and all data should be available across all applications.

Although a centralized database is technologically possible, the factory of the future will probably maintain a distributed database because of the capabilities of minicomputer and microprocessor technology. This technology, along with local area networking, permits efficient transfer of files between databases, provides greater flexibility and responsiveness at the machine and process level where the transformation process occurs.

It is important that future applications be easy to modify and reconfigure. Information systems should anticipate change. Installing an application package should not require undesired changes to the activity. At the other extreme, an application package should not automate chaos. Configurable software requires the process for which the computer system is written to be evaluated to determine the best way to operate before the system is developed. It also requires the application to be flexible to achieve a form and fit that can be enhanced easily over time by operational personnel.

Future capabilities will include interconnected enterprise management systems with high-capacity, secure data transport; intelligent terminals and workstations; and database transfer throughout the enterprise. Companies will integrate these features and add artificial intelligence and knowledge-based systems, object-oriented systems, and real-time update.

The services of the knowledge worker will be in high demand around the world. Knowledge workers are easy to recognize. Their work environment tends to be quiet and tastefully decorated, often within tall steel-and-glass buildings. When they are not analyzing, designing, or developing strategies, they are in meetings or on the telephone giving advice or making deals.

Routine production workers can become knowledge workers by using advanced technologies and being given the responsibility to alter how their activity is performed to increase productivity. Production workers who have broader responsibilities and more control over how production is organized cease to be routine workers—becoming knowledge workers at a level very close to the production process.

COST MANAGEMENT IMPLICATIONS

The late 1980s represented a watershed period for cost accounting. The recent emergence of cost management is a direct result of companies' trying to manage 1990s manufacturing enterprises with a 1920s accounting system. Businesses have become increasingly aware of its shortcomings. Articles on the subject have appeared in virtually every business magazine.

The dramatic changes in manufacturing suggest a time of transition for cost accounting—a prelude to new cost management approaches. Accounting must become more than simply recording, summarizing, and reporting the financial aspects of business operations. The cost management domain must maximize enterprise rather than functional performance. Through activity management the basic functional activities and their interrelationships are readily perceived to ensure that they accomplish the fundamental goals of the enterprise.

What is quite unusual about this moment is not its coming, but its arrival in so many parts of the company at the same time—manufacturing, engineering, management, and accounting. Many companies, at different levels of technology deployment and in different industries, are now simultaneously seeking to revise old concepts and question conventional truths.

These companies are demanding that the new cost management systems determine a cost that mirrors the manufacturing process, identifies waste, isolates cost drivers, and provides visibility of cost reduction/performance improvement opportunities. The profitability of a product over its life cycle becomes an important focus, characterized by full-stream tracking of costs as incurred, from inception to retirement.

Another major type of change is the shift in emphasis from a fixed/variable distinction in contribution analysis to traceability. Direct labor will continue to decrease as a component of product cost, approaching a fixed cost in nature. Hence there will be a minimum of variable costs beyond material. In the new environment the traceability of cost becomes more critical than the traditional distinction between variable and fixed. The new decision support systems will be built on traceability. Improved traceability will result in fewer arbitrary allocations and erode the distinction between direct and indirect costs.

Nonfinancial performance measures will achieve a level of importance equal to financial measures. Strategies such as time compression in product delivery systems require an ongoing monitoring of time. Process balance will be more important than machine usage; quick response to the marketplace becomes more important than machine usage or labor efficiencies. New performance measures will be developed at the activity level. Measures of capacity costs become critical. Bottlenecks in the product delivery system, whether in manufacturing or customer service, must be identified and evaluated as cost drivers. Companies must be able to measure improvements in the velocity of the manufacturing process, new product development, distribution, and customer service.

Life-cycle management becomes important. Cost accounting systems have focused primarily on the cost of physical production, without accumulating costs over the entire design, manufacture, market, and support cycle of a product.

Activities related to the development of products and the manufacturing process represent a sizeable investment of capital. The benefits accrue over many years and, under conventional accounting, are not directly identified with the product being developed. They are treated instead as a period expense, buried in overhead, and allocated to all products (typically as direct labor). Many companies use life-cycle models for planning and budgeting new products, but they fail to integrate these models into existing cost accounting systems. It is important to provide feedback on planning effectiveness and the impact of design decisions on operational and support costs.

Period reporting hinders management decisions. Shorter product life cycles result in less latitude for management error, since the cost recovery periods are short. Today's cost accounting systems are based on period reporting and do not provide life-cycle reporting. This hinders management's understanding of product-line profitability and the potential cost impact of long-term decisions such as engineering design changes.

Life-cycle costing and reporting provide management with a better picture of product profitabiltiy and help managers gauge the effectiveness of their planning activities.

Finally, cost management will be closely intertwined with corporate culture. The introduction of cost management has run into severe political sensitivities. While managers concede that the information in a cost management system is superior to that of existing techniques, they come up with many reasons for inertia. They ask questions such as: "What other companies have implemented the system?" or "What software is available?" The cost of mismanagement is not obvious!

SUMMARY

The decline of traditional manufacturing and accounting marks a historic departure. It also provides significant opportunities for creativity and innovation in investment and corporate management.

The progressive use of advanced manufacturing technology and information systems made the traditional cost system obsolete by creating a computer- and overhead-intensive environment. However, the majority of cost accounting systems are still driven by direct production volume (labor, machine hours, material) and provide minimal guidance for controlling overhead.

This change has raised challenges to the relevance and appropriateness of almost all the systems and procedures in place at businesses and the concepts that managers have learned during their university training.

Although recognizing the problem is a good beginning, the pressing need now is for solutions. Companies are struggling with the question of how to align their cost management system with the operating environment while instilling a philosophy of continual improvement. The challenge is to *perform all activities correctly the first time*. New cost management systems are being proposed as a solution to this problem.

3

ACTIVITIES, ACTIVITY ACCOUNTING, AND COST MANAGEMENT

The purpose of this chapter is to:

- Define and contrast activities, activity accounting, business processes, and cost management
- Describe a transaction process model for defining activities
- Describe the key characteristics that provide a basis for evaluating the effectiveness of activities
- Provide an overview of the key components of an activity accounting and cost management system

This book is about activities; more specifically about managing activities to gain and sustain a competitive advantage. An *activity* is a combination of people, technology, raw materials, methods, and environment that produces a given product or service. It describes *what* an enterprise does: the way time is spent and the outputs of the process. Examples of activities include:

- Closing a sale
- Producing marketing material
- Assembling the final product
- Billing the customer

Ultimately, an enterprise can manage only what it does—its activities. The starting point for managing activities is to understand the resources currently assigned to today's activities (activity cost), the volume of output (activity measure), and how well the activity is performed (performance measure). This information is derived from the activity accounting system.

Activity accounting is a process of accumulating and tracing cost and performance data to a firm's activities and providing feedback of actual results against the planned cost to initiate corrective action where required. It is a tool for understanding cost. An activity accounting system assigns costs as they actually exist at a point in time—not as they should or could be performed.

Cost management uses activity cost and performance information to guide formulation of strategic plans and operational decisions and identify improvement opportunities. A cost management system uses activity cost and performance information to determine a product cost that mirrors the manufacturing enterprise and to challenge what costs should be.

ACTIVITY HIERARCHY

Activities form the foundation of cost management systems. An activity describes the way an enterprise employs its time and resources to achieve corporate objectives. Activities are processes that consume substantial resources to produce an output. The principal function of an activity is to convert resources (materials, labor, and technology) into outputs (products). For instance, the primary activities of a manufacturing engineering department include developing and maintaining bills of material, developing and maintaining routing, filling special orders, conducting capacity studies, suggesting process improvement, and designing tools.

A *function* is an aggregation of activities that are related by a common purpose, such as material procurement, security, and quality. Although most companies are organized functionally, the total spectrum of activities related to the function is much broader than the organizational unit that has primary responsibility for the function. For example, the responsibility for certain quality activities is assigned to the quality department. Yet many other quality activities, such as quality planning for product design, in-process inspection, rework, and customer service, occur in other departments. There is no requisite interdependency among the activities in a function other than relating to a common purpose.

A *business process* is a network of related and interdependent activities linked by the outputs they exchange. The activities are related because a specified event initiates the first activity in the process, which in turn triggers subsequent activities. An output or information flow occurs where two activities interact. The exchange of an output or information flow draws a boundary between different activities within a process and links them in a strong cause-and-effect relationship. Activities are defined in terms of the information elements necessary to perform them and to create their output.

A *task* is the combination of work elements, or operations, that makes up an activity—in other words, a task is how the activity is performed. Several different organizations might accomplish the same activities using significantly different tasks. An *operation* is the smallest unit of work used for planning or control purposes.

Activities, rather than functions or tasks, were chosen as the basis of cost management because they are at the appropriate level of detail to support an ongoing accounting system. Reporting at the function level is too global to trace costs accurately, whereas reporting at the task level is too insignificant (localized) for control. For example, to report the task of data entry of time cards into a payroll system separately from the processing of payroll checks would provide minimal value on an ongoing basis. For this reason, activities are used to document an organization's operations.

The hierarchical relationship of functions, business processes, activities, tasks, and operations is graphically outlined in the following list:

Function:	Marketing and sales
Business process:	Sell product
Activity:	Propose on job
Task:	Prepare proposal
Operation:	Type proposal
Information element:	
	Customer
	Part number
	. . .
	. . .
	. . .
	Due date

A function is *what gets done*, whereas an activity is *what the enterprise does* to accomplish the function. For example, a salesperson's selling of a product is an activity within the sales and marketing function. The activity of selling a product is distinct from the activity of pricing the product, yet both are part of the sales and marketing function. A salesperson might perform a myriad of activities including selling a product, pricing a product, and processing an order.

The business process of selling a product might consist of activities such as traveling to the customer, making a presentation, preparing a proposal, and following up. An example of a task is typing a letter to a potential customer or making travel arrangements.

ACTIVITY OVERVIEW

Activities are defined in the broadest sense to include both manufacturing processes (those processes that transform raw materials into finished products) and the myriad of actions that support the manufacturing process. Activities transcend all steps within the chain of value—product design, manufacturing engineering, production, distribution, marketing, and after-sales service.

Accounting based on activities therefore provides equal visibility for support and production costs. All traditional cost accounting textbooks begin by defining product cost as the sum of direct labor, direct material, and overhead. Activity accounting requires no such arbitrary distinctions between direct and indirect costs. The manufacturing process is described in terms of product-related activities including those that do not physically touch the product. Production activities can be thought of as execution of the process plan in accordance with the production schedule. Material is purchased, labor and machines are assigned to build products.

Activities that occur in support departments and those that occur on the shop floor are highlighted equally because the major activities of all organizational units are identified. A primary criterion of activity accounting is the ability to trace an activity to a product, process, **project**, or other reporting objective for which management needs cost information.

Activities are performed by people or by automated processes. Too often managers focus on controlling people-related costs to the detriment of automated activities. In defining activities, think of time as a series of activities or tasks to be completed. Time is an attribute of both people-related activities and automated activities.

Activity definition is independent of the specific organization. Activities represent what is done in an enterprise. Every manufacturing enterprise must perform many of the same basic activities to function. Depending on the size of the company, activities may be performed by specialized workers or by more general workers who perform multiple activities. However, the activities must be performed in small as well as in large companies. What varies is the degree of specialization and responsibility for decisions.

Activity Elements

It is useful to characterize an activity by reducing it to its simplest form—the processing of a transaction. A transaction process is described in terms of its resources, inputs, outputs, and procedures, as illustrated in the following diagram:

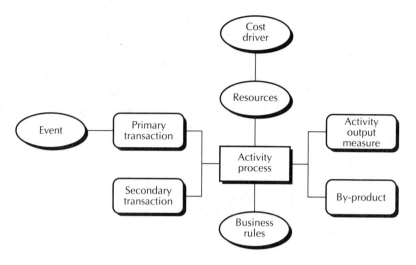

An *event* is the consequence or result of an action external to the activity. Events trigger the execution of an activity. The two primary types of events are a clock event and an external event. A clock event occurs regularly. An external event occurs outside the activity.

Transactions are used as surrogates for activities and business events. A *transaction* is a physical (including electronic) document associated with the transmittal of information. The document serves as evidence of the transaction. The receipt of a customer order, for example, would trigger an order entry activity. The output of the activity would be a computerized customer order transaction. Other examples of transactions include:

- Purchase order
- Labor tracking record
- Material receipt
- Work order

Transactions normally occur at the start or completion of an activity and are the output of key events. For example, a machine breakdown results in a maintenance repair order. The event was the machine breakdown, but the maintenance repair order transaction is an excellent surrogate for the event.

To illustrate the use of transactions, consider the activities associated with receiving material:

Activity	Transaction	Recorded by	Resulting Activities
Receive material	Material receipt	Person at dock via CRT	Receive material Inspect material Move material Store material Pay for material Retrieve material

The material receipt transaction is a means of charging the cost of the receiving department for the specific material received. These costs are then traced to products and used to evaluate the efficiency and effectiveness of the purchasing department and to make decisions about whether to buy in large quantities.

An activity requires resources to accomplish its objective. *Resources* are the factors of production—labor, technology, travel, supplies, and the like—employed to perform an activity. Examples of resources include the following:

Activity	**Resource**
Sell car	Car Salesman Showroom
Service car	Skilled mechanic Tools Service manual Garage

Typical resources include money, credit, capital, land, property, facilities, technology, and people.

Resources are purchased externally or obtained from other departments; that is, the output of one activity becomes an input (resource) to another activity. An activity cost is the sum of all resources including inputs from other internal activities.

An activity's *cost behavior pattern* is the manner in which the resources vary in relation to changes in the number of occurrences of the activity.

An *input* to an activity includes the physical documents that trigger the activity or supply information. Inputs, as well as outputs, are expressed as a physical unit such as a transaction. Inputs emanate from either an internal or external supplier.

Many inputs are required to perform an activity, but only one event triggers its execution while other inputs supply information. The action of a trigger can be stated as, "When this event occurs, start this activity." The issue of a purchase order, for example, is triggered by the receipt of a material request. The single triggering input (transaction) is important to manage because its occurrence triggers the execution of the activity. Additional information is supplied by the purchasing specifications and a vendor list.

In an accounting sense the input transactions constitute the objective and verifiable evidence of consummated business transactions. Characteristically, the input is consumed by the activity process and converted to an output.

A *cost driver* is a factor that creates or influences cost. Cost driver analysis identifies the cause of cost. For example, the factory layout is a key determinant of the cost of material movement and work-in-progress. A plant organized into groups of similar machines requires a significant amount of material movement. On the other hand, a cellular manufacturing layout concentrates all the machinery necessary to build a part in a single location to minimize material movement and work-in-progress.

A positive cost driver results in revenue, production, or support-related activities that generate profit. For example, a customer sale creates the need to:

- Prepare a sales order
- Produce a production order

A negative cost driver causes unnecessary work and reduced profitability. For example, a customer complaint creates a need to:

- Redeliver the product
- Perform field service

An *output* is the culmination (product) of the transformation of resources by an activity. It is what the user receives or what the activity produces. It is the result or objective of performing the activity. Examples of outputs include the following:

Activity	Output
Bill customer	Invoice
Advertise product	Advertisement
Assemble final product	Finished chair

It is important to keep in mind that the output is the result of the activity, *not* the goal (for example, an activity to sell a car results in a sales contract, not the profit that is the goal). The execution of an activity therefore creates certain tangible documents or an intangible action, idea, or concept. The product of an activity is its *activity measure*, which is gauged in terms of "number of activity occurrences per period."

There is always an expected product of an activity such as an accounting statement, payroll checks, machined parts, or packaged products. The activity may occasionally produce a **by-product**.

The output of an activity is intended to meet customers' demands. The customer in this sense is not only the final consumer of product or service, but also the next user of the output of an activity.

An activity's output becomes an input to other activities, an external customer, or a product. The completion of the purchase order, for example, is an event that triggers a subsequent activity to receive the material.

The *process* is the manner in which the activity is performed. It encompasses all the systematic tasks and operations that contribute to the transformation of inputs into outputs. A process can be performed in numerous ways with different factors of production. The resources involved in scheduling production manually or with the aid of a computer system are quite dissimilar, yet they are alternative methods of one scheduling process. The terms *activity* and *process* are often used interchangeably.

An enterprise establishes control procedures for activities that regulate the transformation of input into output. *Control* is the regulation of a process to ensure a predictable output of uniform quality. Controls regulate the flow of data, prescribe operating logic, and establish parameters and tolerances.

Activities are controlled by business rules. A *business rule* defines the goals, strategies, and regulations governing the activity. Rules take the form of policies, procedures, rules of thumb, and algorithms. Policy is essential to translate high-level enterprise objectives into detailed plans. For example, the business rules for the activity of scheduling production orders might be to accumulate several orders into a batch when determining machining sequence. These procedural rules are typically embedded in scheduling techniques.

Business rules are not changed by the activity to which they apply. For example, an activity to issue material depends on whether the material is in stock. If there is no material, then the activity to issue material is suspended. However, the business rules that govern the issue of material are independent of the material's availability.

Business rules are developed from two forms of knowledge: basic and expert. Basic knowledge is based on known relations such as time and cost. Expert knowledge is derived from experience.

Activity Classifications

1. Activities are repetitive or nonrepetitive. A *repetitive activity* is what the organization does on a continual basis. Repetitive activities have consistent input, output, and processing and are managed within the activity accounting system. For example, initially identifying a vendor is different from selecting a vendor for a particular order. Both activities involve unique repetitive processes. Because each represents a significant commitment of resources, they are separate activities. As such they represent a defined area of accountability.

A *nonrepetitive activity* is a one-time activity. Nonrepetitive activities are managed within a **project management** system. The latter often demands a business process analysis approach since, by their nature, nonrepetitive activities are one-time projects and often span several departments.

2. Activities are either primary or secondary. A *primary activity* contributes directly to the mission of a department or organizational unit. Designing and modifying products are two of the primary activities of an engineering department. They are the reasons the engineering department was created. A characteristic of a primary activity is that its output is used outside the organization or by another organization within the company.

A *secondary activity* supports an organization's primary activities. Secondary activities are general activities such as administration, supervision, training, and secretarial work carried out in support of the whole or part of an organizational unit's primary activities. The employees in an engineering department, for example, are not hired to be trained, complete timesheets, or attend meetings.

Secondary activities support only a single department and should increase the efficiency and effectiveness of the primary activities in that department. Although these activities are essential to the effective execution of primary activities, they drain time and resources from the primary activities and must be carefully managed. A common characteristic of secondary activities is that they are consumed by the primary activities in an organization.

Secondary activities should be carefully scrutinized to determine whether they are necessary. The ratio of secondary activities to primary activities is an indication of an organizational unit's bureaucracy. For example, consider the activities of a loan officer on the following page.

This 85/15 ratio is considered very good. Suppose, however, that all loan officers' ratio of primary activities to secondary activities is 50/50, and that the current level of effort is 250 person-years for the primary activities and 250 person-years for the secondary activities. If half of the secondary activities are shifted to (lower-paid) clerical staff, the net savings to the organization will be dramatic. The 125 person-years of loan officer secondary effort

Primary Activities	Time (%)	Secondary Activities	Time (%)
Business Development		Customer file maintenance	1
Sales calls—existing customers	20	Cross-selling	1
Sales calls—new customers	20	Loan operations	5
Commercial loan negotiation	5	Community involvement	3
Commercial loan checking	5	Internal reporting	1
Customer Service		Budgeting	1
Servicing commercial loan portfolio	20	Training	2
Loan review	5	Employee relations	1
Loan pricing	5	Total	15
Loan review documentation	5		
Total	85		

could be performed by 88 dedicated clerical staff. This can result in considerable savings, as shown here with some representative salaries:

$$
\begin{array}{lclr}
125 \text{ person-years at } \$55,000 & = & \$6,875,000 \\
88 \text{ person-years at } \$30,000 & = & -\$2,640,000 \\
\hline
& & \$4,235,000
\end{array}
$$

3. An activity is either required or discretionary. A *discretionary activity* is optional, depending on the manager's judgment.

4. It is important to determine the degree of influenceablity of an activity. Many factors influence an activity's performance. External factors are, in general, less influenceable than internal factors. Weather or regulatory requirements are examples of external factors. Company policy and procedures are examples of internal factors.

5. Activities also vary in their degree of leverage in the marketplace. For example, the activity of designing a product has a high degree of leverage: Some designs clearly promote product desirability. A goal of being the lowest cost per design-hour is not an appropriate goal. Complying with external regulations, on the other hand, has a low degree of leverage in the marketplace. Meeting external requirements at the lowest cost is an excellent goal. These activities, known as compliance/oversight activities, sustain stewardship responsibility. A second category of low-leverage activities comprises transaction-related activities. These activities reflect the effort needed to process volumes of transactions. A prudent manager will maximize the efficiency of performing these activities. A third category comprises administrative activities. These activities support service work activities; examples include MIS and secretarial. Non-value added activities form a fourth category. These activities correct or revise some form of deficiency. Prudent managers will seek to eliminate or minimize these activities.

Activity Considerations

In structuring an activity, a business has a range of choices to make between different processing methods and resources. Each alternative method of accomplishing an activity will bring with it certain implications for the business in terms of response to markets, manufacturing capabilities, level of investment required, unit cost, and type of control and management structure. The fundamental rationale for choosing a specific method of performing an activity is that it is best able to support the business objectives.

It is difficult to optimize enterprise performance because many activities overlap. Too many things have to be dealt with simultaneously. As a result, the wrong activities are given priority; less important activities consume an inordinate amount of time as actions are ruled by the daily schedule and sidetracked by unimportant matters.

Because the business environment is dynamic, the mix of activities must also be dynamic. When product volumes increase or decrease, for example, companies should ideally revise their activities in keeping with the new level of volume. It is common for costs to increase easily with a higher level of sales yet move down slowly when sales decrease. Too often, companies do not revise activities in a timely manner because the existing accounting systems do not monitor activities and their corresponding cost behavior patterns.

It is interesting to note that traditional accounting systems are indirectly based on activities. The reason is that most organizations are structured around clusters of specialists who perform related activities. Thus the purchasing activities are performed within the purchasing department, manufacturing methods are studied by the industrial engineering department, and so forth. However, clustering by specialty provides a homogeneous grouping of cost to only a limited degree since the cost behavior patterns of each separate departmental activity are dissimilar enough to cause product cost distortion.

BUSINESS PROCESS OVERVIEW

A business process is an orderly arrangement of activities operating under a set of procedures in order to accomplish a specific objective such as marketing products, developing new products, or processing customer orders. The activities are related because a specific event initiates the first activity in the process, which in turn triggers subsequent activities.

An important feature of business processes is that they transcend organizational boundaries. For example, the introduction of a new product would require a marketing assessment of needs, a design for the product, specifications for the manufacturing process, and the development of a bill of materials. This requires effort on the part of marketing, research and development, engineering, manufacturing engineering, and finance.

A business process can be a part of a larger business process. For example, several business processes are part of a customer order business process. The key processes include:

- Material acquisition
- Production scheduling
- Product manufacture
- Product delivery

A business process view of cost is an essential adjunct to the traditional **organization structure**, which equates management and accountability with a vertical manager/subordinate responsibility structure. The traditional structure often leads to inappropriate competition among departments. Engineering thinks that marketing is interested only in selling products no matter how complex the design; marketing thinks that the people in manufacturing are unresponsive; and the finger-pointing goes on.

Anyone who has worked in a manufacturing company can cite examples when engineering, marketing, manufacturing, and financial activities were not coordinated in the introduction of a new product. For example, the business process to introduce a new product would set the following activities in motion:

Activity	Responsible Department
Market analysis	Marketing
Product R&D	R&D
Product design	Engineering
Prototype development	Engineering
Product design testing	Engineering
Quality planning	Quality assurance
Make/buy analysis	Industrial engineering
Process planning	Manufacturing engineering
Financial analysis	Finance

In a typical scenario, the financial people were surprised by the additional inventory required; marketing insisted on releasing the product before it was fully engineered; manufacturing had to spend excessive amounts of money in overtime to get the product out and make up for inadequate engineering time. The productivity of the entire organization was affected when the new product was introduced but was not well tested and, as a result, got a poor customer reaction.

Business process analysis focuses management attention on the interdependencies of departments. It forces managers to realize that their customers are other departments and the performance of their activities impacts subsequent activities in the business process. It is important that the firm extend its definition of the business processes to include links between a firm and its suppliers and customers with a view to reducing costs or enhancing differentiation.

With business process reporting individual department managers are not penalized for "exceeding budget" if overall enterprise costs are lowered. For example, a maintenance department exceeded its capital budget by $75,000 because certain repairs that were formerly contracted out were brought in-house. However, the change resulted in cost savings of over $500,000 in a downstream department. The business process reporting portrayed the wisdom of this choice.

KEY COMPONENTS OF AN ACTIVITY ACCOUNTING SYSTEM

New cost management systems are built on activity information. The advantages of activity management are:

- Setting more realistic cost and performance targets derived from the strategic plan
- Identifying wasteful activities and factors that drive cost
- Improving the quality of pricing, make/buy, and estimating decisions by knowing an accurate product cost (which is derived by tracing the cost of activities to products)

A cost management architecture that ties these approaches together is shown on the following page.

The seven steps to computing activity cost are as follows:

1. Activity analysis
2. Life-cycle classification
3. Determination of activity cost
   a. Tracing of organizational resources to activities with an established causal relationship

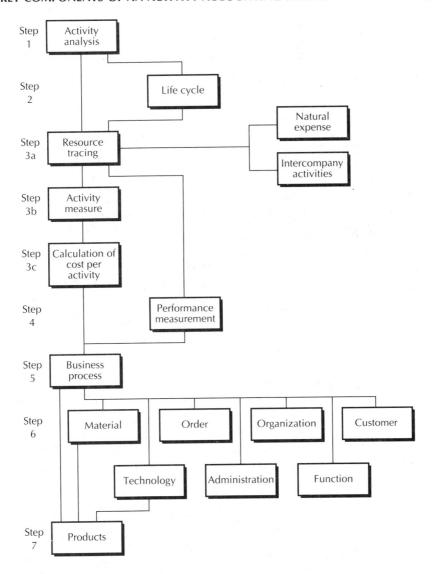

    b. Determination of the measure of activity by which the cost of a given activity varies most directly (as in number of purchase orders, number of hours of grinding, and so forth)

    c. Calculation of cost per activity

4. Identification of performance measures

5. Determination of the cost of business processes

6. Tracing of cost to reporting objective

    a. Technology
    b. Orders
    c. Customers
 7. Calculation of product cost

Activity Analysis

Activity analysis identifies the significant activities (both production and support) of an enterprise in order to establish a basis for accurately determining their cost and performance. Activity analysis decomposes a large, complex organization into elemental activities that are understandable and easy to manage. The explicit management of activities gives an enterprise a better insight into how resources are employed and whether the activity contributes to the achievement of corporate objectives. This approach is in contrast to today's accounting systems, which provide visibility of total resources employed by each organizational unit, but *not* of what the unit *does* (output).

Life-cycle Analysis

Life-cycle analysis provides a framework for managing the cost and performance of a product/process over the duration of its activities. The life cycle commences with the initial identification of a consumer need and extends through planning, research, design, development, production, evaluation, use, logistics support in operation, retirement, and disposal. Life cycle is important to cost control because of the interdependencies of activities in different time periods. For example, the output of the design activity has a significant impact on the cost and performance of subsequent activities.

When costs are not properly matched with time periods, product cost is distorted and cost control disjointed. Traditional accounting systems expense many costs associated with start-up, field operations, maintenance, product support and retirement and disposal which should be capitalized and matched to the products that benefit.

Activity Cost

Activity cost is derived by tracing the cost of all significant resources to perform an activity. The resources consist of people, machines, travel, supplies, computer systems, and other resources that are customarily expressed as cost elements within a chart of accounts.

Activity cost is expressed in terms of a measure of activity volume by which the costs of a given process vary most directly. For example, the cost of scheduling production orders may be expressed as a cost per production order. Measuring activity effectiveness requires knowing the amount of output (activity volume) as well as the activity cost.

Activity Performance Measurement

Performance measures are the financial and operational statistics used to gauge the performance of a company. Under activity-based performance measurement, each activity is analyzed to determine how effectively the work is being performed as gauged by key performance measures such as quality, cost, and time. Each performance measure is simply a different attribute of an activity.

Performance measures provide an important perspective on how effectively the activity helps to achieve enterprise objectives. Performance measures are interrelated. A reduction in time, for example, will impact cost, quality, and flexibility because it impacts the performance of the activity. A key to effective cost management is the implementation of changes that simultaneously improve multiple dimensions of performance.

Technology Accounting

Technology accounting is a system that aims to identify and monitor all significant **technology costs** (plant, equipment, and information systems) and to assign them to products that use the technology. Technology consists of more than machines; it includes the techniques of operation and the organization that makes a particular machine workable. In essence, a technology reflects an evolution of enterprise structure spawned from external market demands and internal decisions. Since technology costs are both a significant determinant of product cost and a key factor in corporate strategy, technology accounting treats production technology costs as a direct cost on the same level as direct labor and direct materials.

Business Functional Analysis

Business functional analysis aggregates the total cost of activities common to a business function. This is accomplished by classifying activities into business functions. Business function costing provides visibility of costs that would otherwise be hidden in numerous departments. The knowledge that the requirement for a given activity resulted from a source outside the department is valuable in understanding what drives a department's normal activities.

Business Process Analysis

A business process analysis determines the interdependencies among activities. Insight into these interrelationships provides visibility of the events that trigger the business process. By controlling the initiating event, a company can reduce or eliminate the cost of all subsequent activities. Today's cost accounting systems do not portray the interrelationships among activities.

Understanding activity relationships facilitates the streamlining of business processes by identifying redundant and unnecessary activities, which increase cost without any corresponding benefit in the marketplace. The entire business process can therefore be restructured to reduce cost and improve efficiency.

The procedure for analyzing a business process is to determine the sequence of activities by following the flow of information from one activity to another. The information flows represent inputs and outputs and constrain an activity. Until information needed to perform an activity is delivered correctly and at the appropriate time, an activity cannot be effectively performed.

Business process analysis facilitates the evaluation of alternative organizational structures. It is often best to organize people and machines into natural groups around processes or information flows.

Activity Product Cost

In activity accounting, the execution of an activity is understood to consume resources. Products consume activities. Product cost is determined through a bill of activities that itemizes the activities and the quantity of each activity consumed in manufacturing a specific product. An activity product cost is derived by summing the cost of all the activities in the bill of activities. Product costing is enhanced by more direct tracing of support costs, which have traditionally been lumped into overhead and allocated to products.

KEY COMPONENTS OF A COST MANAGEMENT SYSTEM

Activity accounting is the foundation of a cost management system. The focus of activity accounting is to understand the cost and performance of significant activities and trace the activities to final cost objectives such as products, customers, and functions. In other words, activity accounting determines the pattern of activity resource use. It doesn't question whether an activity should be performed or if it could be performed more effectively.

Cost management is the analysis of activities to determine the best mix of activities and the optimal level of resources assigned to activities. Some of the important elements of a cost management architecture are discussed here.

Activity Investment Management

Activity investment analysis evaluates the impact of changing an activity process, such as introducing a new technology, on the cost, performance, and interdependencies of activities. The analysis process systematically decomposes the company objectives and strategies into activity level goals that provide a foundation for judging the value of an investment. This facilitates measurement of the cost and nonfinancial performance impacts of the investment by defining the base line set of activities against which to measure change.

Activity investment management embraces the concept of continual improvement by routinely challenging how activities are performed. It decreases the probability of selecting and implementing an inappropriate investment by evaluating capital investments relative to "efficient operations" rather than to existing cost structures. It links investment opportunities to strategic objectives and couples the accounting system with the investment analysis to facilitate corrective action.

Cost Driver Analysis

Cost driver analysis identifies activities that influence the cost and performance of subsequent activities. By reducing or eliminating the event that triggers the first activity in the chain, it may eliminate the need for all subsequent activities. For example, the detection of a defective part requires the part to be reworked or scrapped, the cause of the defect to be corrected, the problem documented, and other related activities. By eliminating the cause—the defective part—the need to perform *all* subsequent activities is eliminated because they are executed *only* when a defective part occurs. Costs are thus reduced.

There are hundreds of activities that occur in even the smallest manufacturing company. Of all these activities only a handful of cost drivers are critical and have a significant impact on the success of a company. By identifying the cost drivers of a business process or an activity, a company can most effectively control costs.

Activity Budgeting

Assessing the factors that control activity volume is an important technique for budgeting the resources necessary to perform an activity. For example, one division of an electronics firm required 15 expeditors, whereas a sister division with a similar revenue required only six. At first glance it appears that the second division's performance was significantly better. However, when one looks at factors such as the numer of parts, number of vendors, and complexity of the manufacturing process, the reason for the difference in support department size becomes evident. The first division had many differentiated products that required significantly more expediting support than the sister division, which had a few high-volume products.

Understanding the number of activity occurrences is an effective tool in predicting the effect on support costs of different strategic decisions. For example, the impact of a 10 percent increase in revenue on a department's budget depends on whether the increase comes from additional sales for a high-production-volume product line or from a low-volume product line. A low-volume product line requires significantly more support cost than a high-volume line.

Non–Value Added Analysis

Non–value added activities result in profitless expense of time, money, and resources and add unnecessary cost to the products. A non–value added analysis identifies activities that can be eliminated with no deterioration of enterprise performance (cost, function, quality, perceived value). Non–value added analysis highlights wasteful activities.

Best-Practice Analysis

A best-practice analysis compares activity cost and performance between different departments, divisions, suppliers, and/or competitors to identify the most efficient way to perform an activity. Once the activities with lowest cost and highest performance are identified, they can be analyzed to identify the source of excellence. The results of the analysis can then be shared with other groups within the company that perform the activity to determine the applicability to their operations.

Activity Target Cost Analysis

Activity target cost analysis determines activity cost and performance goals based on market demand for a product. Target costs are derived by estimating the market price necessary to capture a certain market share and then subtracting the desired profit margin. Typically, a target cost is lower than the initial estimated cost to build a product. The challenge is to reduce the production cost to the target level. Activities provide an excellent basis for identifying opportunities to achieve targets. Identification of non–value added activities and best practices provides a basis to apply value engineering techniques to eliminate or improve the cost and performance of these activities.

Activity Strategic Analysis

Activity strategic cost analysis uses activity cost and performance data to develop enterprise strategies. Strategic cost analysis evaluates a company's activities, from design to distribution, and determines where value to the customer can be enhanced or costs lowered.

Cost management systems play a critical role in allowing a firm to assess the financial impact of various alternatives and to select appropriate strategies. Information obtained from traditional cost accounting systems is usually inadequate for strategic cost analysis because it does not help the firm understand the behavior of costs from a strategic perspective. It follows that a company's accounting systems must be designed to facilitate strategic cost analysis—a function radically different from traditional record keeping.

SUMMARY

Today's model of collecting costs by chart-of-account classification within organizational structure is providing insufficient visibility of key activities and of economic cause-and-effect relationships between activities.

An activity accounting system is used to calculate a more traceable product cost, to control costs, to integrate strategic planning into the cost management system, and to manage performance as well as costs.

A cost management system provides a set of tools for more effective management of cost and performance. The information provided by a cost management system enables manufacturing managers to solve problems rather than treat symptoms. This is critical because if people don't understand the problem, they won't understand the solution.

An activity accounting system relies on the costing of significant business activities to:

- Provide a natural baseline for describing a manufacturing process
- Provide visibility of non–value added activities
- Understand the underlying cause-and-effect relationships between the factors of production and the manufacturing process
- Identify, evaluate, and implement new activities
- Capture the budgeted and actual cost
- Measure the efficiency and effectiveness of the activity

4

WHY ACTIVITIES?

The purpose of this chapter is to:

- Provide an overview of why activities are an appropriate basis for an activity accounting system
- Provide insight into the potency of activity management for achieving enterprise excellence

Activities are a powerful basis for managing an enterprise. Several characteristics of activities make them such a powerful management tool. This chapter examines the most important of these characteristics.

ACTIVITIES ARE ACTIONS

A management system structured on activities ensures that plans are transmitted to a level at which action can be taken. Activities are what organizations do. To make changes, one must change what people do. Therefore, changes must ultimately be made to activities.

In contrast, the traditional practice of collecting costs by cost element (labor, plant and equipment, supplies, travel, and the like) does not provide the detailed information necessary to identify needed changes. For example, consider labor in the engineering department. Two important activities of a design engineer are to develop new products and redesign existing products for a particular customer (configuration control).

A conventional cost accounting system, which captures the total cost of labor at the departmental level, does not provide insight into how labor is used. To accurately trace costs to products it is necessary to break costs down into activities with unique cost behavior patterns.

The management of new product design and configuration control are two activities of an engineer with significantly different cost behavior patterns, yet they are part of a single salary cost account in the engineering department. The cost behavior pattern of new product design is related to the number and complexity of new product designs. Configuration control, on the other hand, entails product customization to meet the specifications of individual orders. The cost behavior pattern of configuration control is related to the number of one-time orders and the complexity of the change required. Traditional practice would group these separate activities together even though they have separate cost behavior patterns. Activity analysis preserves the individual nature of these two activities.

ACTIVITIES IMPROVE PRODUCT COST ACCURACY

Product cost computed on the basis of direct labor, machine hours, or material cost overhead allocation distorts product cost because it erroneously assumes that the usage of other factors of production are proportional to the direct factor. The cost behavior pattern of the purchase order activity, for example, depends on the number of purchase orders not on the value of the material purchased—a common method of allocating purchase order costs to products. This process overcosts high-value components.

In contrast, activity accounting improves the accuracy of product costing by tracing activities to products on the basis of usage. The number of production orders and order size, for example, allows one to trace activities related to production scheduling directly to units produced.

Under traditional cost accounting, it is common practice to include engineering costs in overhead and allocate them to products on the basis of direct labor. Thus products with the largest proportion of direct labor absorb the bulk of engineering costs. However, products that have been in production for some time have had most of their bugs eliminated and thus require less engineering support. New products, in contrast, typically have more production and quality problems that require a number of engineering changes. Engineering changes are more accurately related to factors such as time in service, product complexity, and use of standardized components—not direct labor content.

Similarly, the cost of processing purchase orders can be traced to products on the basis of the number of purchase orders required to build a part. Products with a significant number of purchased components would receive a higher proportion of purchasing costs than products with few purchased parts, since additional purchasing activity is required. Other activities, such as management and administration, are not directly traceable to products. These costs should be excluded—or allocated if the organization wants a fully absorbed cost.

Activity accounting differentiates products produced in small and large batches. It traces the costs of set-up–related activities to the production order that creates the demand for those activities. The cost of set-up–related activities is then spread to the products generating the batch. Thus low-volume products incur a relatively high set-up cost, whereas high-volume products incur relatively little set-up cost.

In contrast, traditional cost accounting allocates batch-related costs to all products manufactured during the accounting period on an erroneous volume-related basis.

ACTIVITIES DRIVE COST

Cost drivers are factors that cause cost in subsequent activities. Too often cost control is focused at the point of cost occurrence without adequate consideration of cost drivers. Consider the activity of inserting components into electronic boards. One technique to control insertion cost is to minimize the resources allocated to the activity. Direct labor, for example, may be replaced by an automated insertion machine. The resulting lower cost and a more efficient process results in an increase in company profitability. The company has improved its competitiveness; or has it? Perhaps a symptom—high insertion cost—has been treated rather than the cause of the cost.

Consider two key causes of the insertion process—the state of technology and the product design. The current state of technology allows surface mount technology to replace the insertion activity. Rather than increase the efficiency of the insertion activity, an alternative is to invest in surface mount technology. Similarly, the need for the insertion activity might be reduced through the redesign of products. In both cases, the company should address the root causes of the need for insertions *before* attempting to improve its efficiency. In other words, correct the source of the cost rather than treat its symptoms.

Determining the amount of time a design engineer, for instance, spends on various activities, such as new product design or engineering changes, provides a basis for understanding what causes engineering cost. Excessive engineering change might indicate poor integration between the product design and the manufacturing engineering function, which determines how the product will be produced after it has been designed. Similarly, a great deal of new product design might suggest that design engineering is not using group technology standardization techniques, thereby resulting in an excessive number of new part designs. In either case, the economic causes of these two activities are significantly different. Activities highlight the area that drives cost, such as product design, and indicate where action is required. The traditional system does not provide this insight.

ACTIVITIES FACILITATE EVALUATION OF ALTERNATIVES

Determining the cost and performance of an activity permits a comparison with different divisions and other companies within the industry that perform the same activity. The most cost-effective operations can then be studied to specify a set of best practices that can aid other divisions in improving operations.

Activity accounting assesses a company's activities to determine if they are being performed cost effectively in comparison to alternatives both inside and outside the company. Activity accounting enhances the understanding of new process technologies. The introduction of a new technology (such as the flexible manufacturing cell or the computerized production control system) changes the factors of production and the performance of activities. Activity accounting identifies the impact of these changes by focusing on how the activities are performed.

Consider the processing of payroll checks. Currently a company may be processing payroll checks manually. An activity accounting system would routinely calculate a cost per payroll check, identify the time it takes to process a check, and evaluate the quality of the process. An alternative method is to acquire a computerized payroll system. The cost and performance of the manual system would be compared to the computerized system to determine the value of the change in terms of its impact on profitability and performance.

Similarly, the manner in which different manufacturing sites process a payroll check can be compared to determine which site has the best performance. This site can then be studied to determine why it has the best practice.

ACTIVITIES FOCUS CORPORATE STRATEGY

Activities are what an enterprise does. Strategic goals represent what the enterprise wants to achieve. Knowing the corporate goals enables a company to determine what it is doing (activities) and how its activities relate to those goals.

Activities and the mix of products management has chosen to sell must be continuously evaluated to ensure that the activities contribute to the achievement of corporate objectives. Poor structuring of company activities leads to missed deadlines, unfinished projects, disappointed customers, and non–value added costs.

A common corporate objective is to be a low- or lowest-cost producer. However, managers who claim to hold this position rarely know how accurate their own product costs are, much less how they compare with competitors' product costs.

ACTIVITIES COMPLEMENT CONTINUOUS IMPROVEMENT

In daily operations, many activities are non–value added and secondary to the organization's mission. Visibility of these non–value added and secondary activities provided by the cost management system is a basis for continuous improvement.

Activity analysis provides information to identify redundant, duplicate, and wasteful activities together with the factors that drive cost. Understanding activities provides a basis for determining whether to continue performing or to restructure an activity. Continuous improvement has several objectives:

- Elimination of waste (non–value added activities)
- Improvement of performance of value added activities
- Synchronization of lead time within new product introduction and production cycle
- Improvement of quality
- Elimination of process variance by correcting the source cause of the variance
- Simplification of activities

Continual cost reductions do not come automatically with experience or the passage of time. They require constant management attention in all matters to achieve productivity gains and cost reductions. Too often product cost, and consequently price, drift out of line with competitors and products become unprofitable without management's realizing the problem or taking appropriate action until it is too late.

There are several inhibitors to continuous improvement. First, there is an overemphasis on direct manufacturing costs. It is much more important to concentrate on total enterprise costs. Overhead and other support costs can throw a company's cost structure out of line. Support activities tend to overaccumulate in good times when there is no pressure for tight performance and the exercise of common sense.

Second, inflation militates against continuous improvement. Inflation provides a false sense of security that allows companies to pass higher cost to consumers and avoid addressing fundamental cost problems. It is easy to raise prices when cost automatically increases with inflation. This, in turn, leads to lack of discipline in controlling cost.

Activity accounting provides information crucial to continuous improvement. It yields a wealth of information on operating activities that managers can use to eliminate waste.

Activity accounting supports continuous improvement by managing the business processes. Consider the traditional procurement process. The key activities include:

- Production scheduling
- Purchase requisition processing
- Purchase order processing
- Goods received voucher processing
- Supplier invoice processing
- Supplier statement processing
- Supplier payment

The buyer receives a weekly printout of the production plan and material requirements, checks the inventory computer records, and compares the requirements with the quantity on hand. If there is a shortfall, a purchase requisition is created and the buyer calls the vendor to place a purchase order.

When goods are received, they are inspected and moved to raw material stores for further issue to production. A goods received voucher is completed. The supplier issues an invoice, which is entered into the accounts payable system. The supplier issues a statement of all outstanding invoices monthly, which is matched against the purchaser's outstanding invoices. The purchase order is matched with the supplier invoice, and the vendor is paid during the next check-processing cycle.

An activity management system would identify and analyze these activities. The activity analysis provides insight into how to restructure the process. For example, a purchasing department study might conclude that all the activities other than production scheduling and supplier payment are non–value added and could be eliminated. This new procurement process is triggered by the weekly production schedule. The weekly schedule is sent to the supplier, who delivers parts daily in accordance with the schedule. The supplier is paid weekly on the basis of units shipped. As a result, all activities other than production scheduling and supplier payment are eliminated.

ACTIVITIES ARE COMPATIBLE WITH TOTAL QUALITY MANAGEMENT

Total quality management (TQM) means perfect quality in products and services. It emphasizes the importance of quality in every aspect of operations. TQM has two objectives—to make things right the first time and to work for continuous improvement. TQM emphasizes the need to treat all manufacturing functions as processes and strive to improve them. The traditional product cost model—which separately collects labor, material, and cost by product, rather than process—is not compatible with the TQM philosophy; the effect of a process change on a product cost cannot be easily determined. Activities are processes and are therefore compatible with TQM.

ACTIVITY ACCOUNTING IS COST-EFFECTIVE

A cost management system must be only as complex as necessary to achieve the required benefits but not so simple that it fails to provide enough information to support enterprise excellence. To paraphrase Albert Einstein: "A cost management system should be as simple as possible, but no simpler!" Managers who simplify manufacturing operations and eliminate waste do not wish to introduce a product costing system that is excessively costly to design, implement, and operate. The costs of the activity accounting system must not exceed the benefits of the system.

Activity accounting facilitates the understanding of a complex business environment by breaking it down into individual activities. Organizations are continually undergoing changes: evolution of technology, management philosophy, products, and so on. Activity accounting is structured to support change. As activities and factors of production change, the new activities and their associated cost and performance are captured.

Activity accounting can be applied to an entire organization, its production operations, a department, or a work cell. The activity focus permits a flexible cost management system that decouples the organization structure from the functions performed. The decoupling of activities from the organization facilitates an adaptable and flexible **cost accumulation** procedure to support multiple reporting objectives.

An activity accounting system is typically first implemented as a separate management system rather than a replacement for the financial system. This avoids the need to change the accounting model, which is acceptable to auditors and external agencies. For example, today the activities of accounts payable, payroll, and personnel are seldom treated as part of product cost. However, these activities are traceable to products through activity measures such as the number of different raw materials used in a product, number of employees, number of new hires, or number of new products. Rather than being traced to products through the same modified financial system used to support external financial reporting, then, these activities can be traced as part of a separate management accounting system.

ACTIVITIES ARE EASILY UNDERSTOOD BY THE USERS

Activities are "natural" identifiers because they are easily understood by such diverse groups as engineers, operations personnel, accountants, and top management. Activities such as processing payroll checks, inserting components into electronic boards, and testing new products are universally understood throughout the organization. Thus activities provide an effective medium for communication between accounting and operational personnel because they correspond to familiar manufacturing terms and events.

Conversely, much of today's accounting information is presented in financial terms rather than in user terms. For example, when costs are allocated among departments, users do not understand what composes the charge and consequently cannot relate it to the activities and tasks performed. As a result, they often question the fairness of the charge and feel they have little information with which to control cost.

ACTIVITIES LINK PLANNING AND CONTROL

Feedback is essential to control. It is crucial that planning (strategic, decision support, investment, and so on) and control (cost accounting) be linked, because management needs information to make necessary adjustments to achieve the plan or to make modifications to the plan. Anticipating problems is essential.

Today much of the information coming to management is derived from different information systems. Inconsistency among systems complicates the management process of planning, monitoring, and calling attention to problem areas in order to achieve anticipated results. Without a consistent planning and operational control system, it is difficult for managers to achieve their plans.

Activity accounting provides a logical framework ensuring that the control system—as represented by the cost accounting and performance measurement system—is consistent with the planning systems. Activities form the common denominator that links the planning and control processes. In an activity management approach, the company's decision support system and cost management would be activity based.

Knowing an activity cost assists in planning and budgeting. Each organizational unit is analyzed to determine the current activities and cost per activity output. This information represents the current level of service. The impact on the budget of changes in service level can thus be identified.

ACTIVITIES INTEGRATE FINANCIAL AND NONFINANCIAL PERFORMANCE MEASURES

Increasingly competitive advantage accrues to organizations that manage nonfinancial performance by compressing lead time and improving quality. Unfortunately, today, too much attention is focused on short-term financial performance—profit margins, return on capital, and similar measures. An activity accounting system provides a vehicle for evaluating the total performance of an activity, including time, quality, and flexibility.

In activity accounting, performance is measured as the cost per output, time to perform the activity, and quality of the output. Performance measures are monitored to determine their trend, and the people responsible for each activity are made accountable for continually improving the performance.

ACTIVITIES HIGHLIGHT INTERDEPENDENCIES

Activities are interrelated. For example, a product cannot be manufactured until it has been designed. Because most costs are determined by decisions made early in the life-cycle process, it is important to understand the interrelationships among activities.

Today's cost accounting systems do not portray the interrelationships among activities. An understanding of the inputs and outputs of activities clarifies the linkage among activities. This visibility provides insight into the performance of an activity by highlighting its link to the activities that cause it to be executed so that corrective action can be applied to the original cause of cost.

ACTIVITIES FACILITATE
LIFE-CYCLE MANAGEMENT

Life-cycle accounting is defined as the accumulation of cost and performance for activities that occur over the entire life cycle of a product, from inception to abandonment. The life-cycle concept is significantly different from conventional practices, which expense many costs in the current period rather than match them to future products.

Life-cycle accounting requires the separation of accounting practices and risk. Today, risk is managed by expensing costs as incurred. The conventional cost accounting model distorts product costs by expensing a major portion of a product's cost before production begins. It is a common, conservative practice to expense research, development, and all other preproduction costs as incurred.

Accounting for risk by conservatively expensing activities for which a future benefit is planned makes it difficult to measure the success or failure of those expenditures. Significant investment is made in these activities, but the conventional model does not measure the return on that investment. It also encourages people to consider many of these expenditures as discretionary when success in today's marketplace requires continuing investment in research, development, and marketing.

Most agree that engineering a product for ease of production is most efficiently done during the research and development stage of a product's life. Problems are much more easily and efficiently resolved at this time than once the product is being produced.

These preproduction costs directly impact current earnings under the conventional model, encouraging managers to place many products into production prematurely so as to reflect positive short-term performance. Finally, expensing many of these product costs as incurred means that the actual cost of a product is unknown and the product may in fact be selling at a loss while the company reports a profit.

An example of activity-based life-cycle management can be seen in the treatment of engineering changes. Activity accounting traces the costs of engineering change activities to the product for which the change is being made. Traditional product costing, however, allocates engineering cost according to a volume-related measure such as direct labor. This approach allocates an equal amount of engineering cost to each direct labor hour. Products with the most labor hours incorrectly pick up most of the engineering cost. Indeed the process of designing products so as to minimize direct labor results in an inverse relationship between engineering cost and direct labor.

ACTIVITIES IMPROVE DECISION SUPPORT

Activity accounting provides information that gives a realistic picture of the impact of a variety of decisions on current activity consumption. This assists managers in determining production line mix, pricing, developing a make/buy strategy, assessing new technologies, and making other important decisions.

Consider an automotive supplier that expanded its product mix by introducing specialty headlights in order to become a second-source supplier for a large automobile manufacturer. The new product required engineering design, procurement, financial analysis, and other activities. Although introducing this new product did not require hiring a new engineer, purchaser, accountant, it did impact their work load. Over time, as new products were added, the demand for these activities increased to the point where new staff were required. Without visibility of activities, the relationship between these new products and profitability would be obscure.

To be profitable, the new product must show a greater total revenue at the end of its life cycle than the total of *all* directly traceable costs—including R&D and other start-up activities. Traditional systems that use production-related volumes for absorbing overhead spread these costs over all products, including the existing products. The cost system therefore reports that the low-volume specialty products are among the most profitable products sold by the division—an aberration from reality.

An activity accounting system, however, would trace costs to products on the basis of actual activity usage. The resulting product cost shows that low-volume products such as the special headlights were more costly than had been previously thought. Using this information, management was able to consider a range of alternatives—such as dropping certain products, increasing their price, changing their design or other engineering techniques to lower cost—to implement a target cost program to sell the product at a price that will compensate the company for the additional activities required by the product.

SUMMARY

Activity analysis is the set of techniques used to identify the significant activities of an enterprise and analyze their cost and performance in detail. Activities are the heart of a cost management system. Analyzing a firm in terms of activities ensures that plans are transmitted to a level at which action can be taken, facilitates goal congruence, highlights cost drivers, supports continuous improvement, and enhances decision support systems.

5

ACTIVITY ANALYSIS

The purpose of this chapter is to:

- Describe several approaches to activity analysis
- Provide guidelines on aggregating and decomposing activities
- Describe and contrast common techniques for gathering activity information
- Present a seven-step activity analysis methodology

Activity analysis identifies the significant activities of an enterprise to establish a clear and concise basis for describing business operations and for determining their cost and performance. The process of analyzing time use is known as **activity analysis**. It fosters a common understanding of how an enterprise functions in order to improve enterprise performance, including profit, quality, and timeliness. Specifically, activity analysis is used to:

- Understand the current cost and performance of significant activities
- Provide a basis for determining alternative activities to lower cost and/or improve performance
- Provide a basis for improving methods to streamline current activities
- Identify discretionary, secondary, and non–value added activities
- Identify cross-organizational issues

Activity analysis leads to activity management. **Activity management** is the effective and consistent organization of the enterprise's activities in order to use its resources in the best possible way to achieve its objectives. The intent is to change underplanned and externally determined daily operations to goal-oriented and systematically planned ones. Activity management reallocates time and systemizes work methods to improve the effectiveness of activities even in a dynamic environment. Sailors have an old saying: "It doesn't matter in what direction the wind blows; it's important how I set the sails!"

ACTIVITY ANALYSIS OVERVIEW

Activity analysis is used to decompose a large, complex organization into elemental processes (activities) and the outputs of the activities that are understandable and manageable. Activity analysis is based on the observation that an entire system is too large to manage, but its individual components are not.

An activity analysis is an audit of the way companies currently function. Activity analysis leads to activity planning, which determines the resources (and hence skills and staffing levels) required to support a given level of activity service and indicates how business processes can be streamlined by eliminating redundant and wasteful activities.

One objective of activity analysis is to improve enterprise profit and performance by emulating the best practices of an activity performed in several organizations. Such a determination of best practices is possible only if activities are consistently defined among the divisions and departments of a company. A comparison of cost and performance in several organizations that perform a common activity can identify useful similarities in the practices of those organizations. Such a comparison is impossible without a consistent definition of the activity.

AGGREGATION AND DECOMPOSITION

The process of combining activities into functions is referred to as **aggregation**. Aggregating activities common to a function provides a basis for directing management attention to high-cost areas that might otherwise be obscured in numerous individual activities. Functions are analogous to the forest that one views instead of the trees (activities).

The process of breaking down an activity into tasks is referred to as **decomposition**. Essentially, it involves looking inside the activity to model the detailed workings of its internal tasks. Tasks, being the work elements of activities, are at the appropriate level for introducing change. Performance improvement is best achieved by decomposing activities into tasks and then restructuring the tasks.

WHAT IS ANALYZED?

Activity analysis seeks to provide the following information:

- *Activities:* What the enterprise does—specific tasks that make up the job assignment; their relative timing and importance in achieving corporate goals.
- *Input/output:* The transactions that trigger the activity (input) and the product of the activity (output).

No matter which activity analysis technique is used, the same basic information must be obtained, such as the nature of the activities, inputs, outputs, and technologies.

Some of the important information that should be associated with an activity includes:

- Organization unit (**cost center**)
- Business process
- Factors of production
  - Direct material
  - Direct labor
    - Labor hours
    - Labor grade
  - Direct technology
    - Machine type
    - Number of machines
    - Capacity (machine hours)
    - Unit of capacity
    - Description of input/output
    - Sources of input and destination of output
    - Quantity per unit of capacity
  - Facilities
  - Directly traceable overhead expenses
- Time
  - Elapsed
  - Process
- Value added/non–value added indicator
- Quality
- Inputs/outputs
  - Frequency
  - Unit of measure

- Sources of input and destination of output
- Volume

It is important to determine activity workload patterns. The pattern of activity occurrence determines whether most inputs arrive at certain times of the day, month, or year. Understanding the patterns of activity occurrence is important for setting service levels and determining activity capacity.

The evaluation of activities should not be limited to cost alone but should also include performance measures. Performance includes both system performance such as technical characteristics (capacity, size, and weight) and system effectiveness (availability, dependability, and the like). The focus of the activity analysis is on system effectiveness.

Performance measures should be defined for every significant activity. The aim of performance measures is to monitor how the activity is performed in terms of the quality of its output, timeliness (ability to deliver the output at the scheduled time), and flexibility (ability to cope with changes in volume, scope, mix, technology, and requirements).

The resources (factors of production) used to support the execution of an activity are not assigned during the activity analysis stage. Activities are costed after activity definition. Activity costing determines the resources such as capital, people, material, lathes, milling machines, application programs, and personal computers used to support an activity.

Activities are analyzed *as they exist* at the time the analysis is performed—not as they should exist, not as they existed in the past, and not as they exist in similar organizations. If the activity analysis does not reflect the reality of the business, it will be impossible to construct a viable cost management system.

Activity analysis is concerned with facts—information about activities, *not* individual employees. A first-rate activity analysis *must* be the result of a thorough analysis, or it cannot be depended upon as an objective source of activity information.

The activity should be considered a black box, and activity analysis should be concerned only with what it does, not how it works.

ACTIVITY ANALYSIS METHODOLOGY

An activity analysis is a communication tool that provides a set of structured information about what an enterprise does. The activity definitions must provide a logically consistent and demonstrably accurate representation of the totality of the enterprise to be a useful part of the decision-making process. The approach is illustrated in the following diagram:

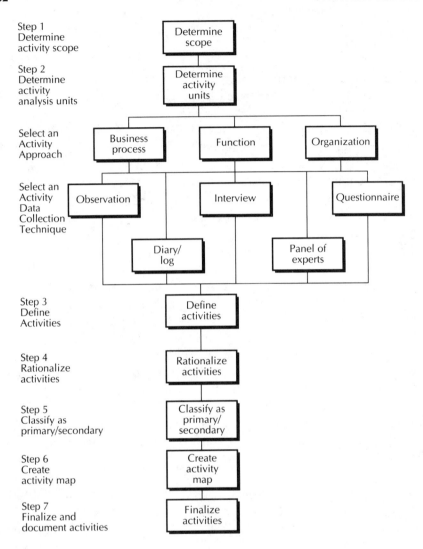

The following sections describe the principal steps required to perform an activity analysis. These steps should be regarded as guidelines, because the specific company environment in which the activity analysis is performed may demand differences in approach.

STEP 1: DETERMINE ACTIVITY ANALYSIS SCOPE

An essential prerequisite to activity analysis is a definition of the specific problem or business decision to be analyzed. A clear statement of definition ensures that the analysis is applied to an area of potential improvement.

Additionally, it limits the range of activities specified in the activity analysis so that the information can be efficiently gathered.

For example, a company faced with competition that uses rapid product introduction as a competitive strategy may apply activity analysis to the process of introducing new products in order to highlight unnecessary and redundant activities. The only activities analyzed would be those impacted by the product introduction process.

STEP 2: DETERMINE ACTIVITY ANALYSIS UNITS

The organizational unit to be analyzed should be divided into groups or departments with a single identifiable purpose. The **activity units** may correspond to organizational units, or they may cross organizational boundaries, since organizational structure is often dictated by political and personal factors rather than functional definitions. Redefining the organizational units into activity units, where appropriate, facilitates a comprehensive and cost-effective analysis.

An organization chart and headcount summary provide a starting point for the process of defining activity units. The purpose of the organization chart and headcount summaries is to ensure that the structure of the organization is fully understood and that the whole organization has been covered. The organization chart is validated with senior management to ensure that it is current and accurately reflects the existing operational structure. Other important information includes flowcharts, department instructions, **fixed asset** registers, facilities' layouts, and other related documentation.

It is important that the activity units be functionally homogeneous and large enough to warrant an analysis. As a rule of thumb, an activity unit should consist of 5 to 20 people with a level of expenditure of $50,000 to $100,000.

STEP 3: DEFINE ACTIVITIES

The next step is to take stock of all the activities performed by an activity unit. There are several techniques for collecting activity data. Each measurement technique is a tool with its own unique advantages and limitations. The primary techniques include the following:

- Analysis of historical records
- Analysis of organizational units
- Analysis of business processes

- Analysis of business functions
- Directed industrial engineering study
- Reconciliation of activity definition

In selecting the appropriate data collection technique, the two key criteria to consider are the degree of precision and the cost of measurement. The more precise measurement techniques require considerable training to apply and, as a general rule, require more time to collect the data. Additional training and analysis time increase the cost of measurement.

Activities should be defined with a noun and a verb. Activity names may be persons, places, or things that play a role in respect to a particular activity. Do not use generic labeling terms such as data, activity, or output. These terms lack the specificity required for activity analysis.

In performing an activity analysis, it is important to use a structured approach. The use of worksheets and work distribution charts helps to analyze time and activities and ensure a consistent analysis. A sample worksheet follows:

No.	Activity	Duration	Input	Output

A work distribution chart summarizes all the activities performed by the employees in a given department. It provides a basis for verifying that all major activities have been recorded and examines the distribution of time to activities. A sample work distribution chart is included at the top of the following page.

3a: Analyze Historical Records

An analysis of historical records involves the use of production statistics compiled over a period of time, perhaps a month or year, to determine what a department does and how long it has taken in the past to process the output of an activity. A starting point for this process is any past activity analysis. In certain cases, an organization might have recently undergone a

Activities	Employee 1	E H	Employee 2	E H	Employee 3	E H	Employee 4	E H	Totals Hrs./%
Orders	Check credit Type invoice	20 12	Check credit Type invoice	18 13	Check credit Type invoice	6 4	Make new file File invoices Pull files	4 8 8	93 59
Adjustments	Account adj.	4	Address change	8	Address change	15	File changes Pull changes	5 5	37 24
Inventory					Inventory control	12	Inventory tickets	6	18 11
Miscellaneous	Order supply File diaries	2 1	Weekly error report	1	Weekly inventory report	2	Search	3	9 6

one-time analysis of its operations as part of a zero-base budgeting, factory analysis, or special project. Alternatively, some individual organizations maintain private labor reports or other local reports that identify activities. Finally, a study of data processing statistics provides insight into activities. Computer operating systems maintain statistics on transaction codes and record volume. This information is an excellent source of activity volume.

3b: Analyze Organizational Units

Activities can be defined by studying the organizational units that perform or manage a functional area to determine how each unit completes its specified objectives. This approach relies to a large extent on various people's knowledge of the company operations.

An organizational analysis normally uses a Delphi approach in defining activities. The **Delphi method** queries the most knowledgeable experts (such as department heads) to identify current activities and the resources allocated to accomplish them. The activities and time allocations recorded are based on the judgment of the experts. The primary Delphi data collection techniques include interviews, questionnaires, panels of experts, and observation. The disadvantage of an organizational definition is that it requires a significant number of loops and rework as business processes and functions are defined.

An organizational analysis is an iterative process of studying individual organizations to develop an initial list of activities and refining the activity definition with subsequent analysis. The seven key steps in an organizational analysis include:

- Analyze job classification
- Review computer records
- Conduct interviews of key personnel
- Observe activities
- Consult panel of experts
- Review diaries and logs
- Review check sheets

1. *Analyze job classification*. An organizational definition of activities starts with an analysis of job classifications. From the organization chart the number of staff assigned to each job classification is extracted in order to calculate the number of full-time equivalent employees. The total hours are broken down by job classification into normal and overtime. The analysis determines what each job classification does and how much time is apportioned to each activity.

During the process a functional description of each organizational unit is developed to identify its mission. Next the staffing level, including job grade/classification is determined. Typically, this information is obtained from staffing charts and job descriptions and validated through interviews with department managers. The activities performed by each job category and the percentage of time spent by each job category on a specific activity are defined.

2. *Review computer records*. The interview is supplemented by a review of the current computer systems that support activities. The review determines the availability and level of data available from the computer system and identifies the frequency of data collection and the integrity of the data.

3. *Conduct interviews of key personnel*. At this point the activity analysis team is ready to begin interviewing, the process of obtaining activity information by questioning the people most directly involved. The biggest advantage of the interview technique is that the direct person-to-person contact usually provides the best understanding of the job. The drawback is that the employee may provide incorrect information. Countless studies have demonstrated that when people's descriptions of their jobs are compared with an actual record of what they do, large differences appear.

A questionnaire is the least expensive method of gathering activity information but provides the least consistency. A questionnaire is effective when used in conjunction with an interview. It allows the respondent to think about the questions that will be asked and to gather any necessary information prior to the interview. Generally speaking, questionnaires are most successful when used by white-collar, managerial, and administrative employees.

An interview checklist serves as a guide to ensure all critical information is analyzed. A sample interview checklist that was developed as part of the General Dynamics–Fort Worth Division activity accounting project follows:

1. Verify organization structure and current staffing.
   - Request a current staffing chart.
   - What are the major classifications of people?
   - Direct/indirect products.
2. What are the major functions of your department?
   - Request any flowcharts or pictures that help illustrate how functions are performed.
2a. Review products list.
   - Are all the products/functions included? If not, please add.
   - Rank products in terms of their importance.
3. What are the most labor-intensive, costly, time-consuming operations/products?
4. What are the bottlenecks? What are the causes of bottlenecks?
5. How do you keep track of the amount of activity in your area?
6. What is your current work load?
7. How do you keep track of your cost/labor?
8. Do you have a workload forecast? How was it developed? How does it vary from time to time and why?
9. Do you have a manpower loading and forecast? How was it developed?
10. What computerized reports and databases are used? What information is input into the system, and how is it done?
11. What information and other support do you need from other organizations that would improve your operations?
12. Provide feedback.

The interview process provides an initial list of significant activities performed by job category. The employee occupation code is a key indicator of the types of activities performed. For each occupation code the key activities and percentage of total time spent on activities is assigned by departmental managers. The percentage of time spent on each activity varies primarily when the activity changes or the level of activity volume changes.

Through the interview process a preliminary definition of activities is developed. The final output of this step is a listing of activities with a narrative text that describes each activity. The magnitude of the acticity is based on estimates of time spent on each activity. For example, a study of occupational codes for a material control department revealed the following:

Labor Grade	Type	Hours
2540	Support	100
2900	Support	300
9050	Direct	1,500
9075	Direct	600
	Total	2,500

Interviews with managers and supervisors determined that the following key activities were performed by the material handling department:

- Incoming material handling
- In-process material handling
- Outgoing material control
- Raw material stores
- WIP stores
- Finished goods stores
- Management and administration
- Training
- Other

These activities were selected because they represent a significant portion of the department's time and cost.

It is important at the outset of the interview process that a standard definition of an activity be established. Different people define different activity models for the same subject area simply because they adopt different points of view. Therefore, the activity definition perspective must be clearly understood by all members of the activity analysis team so that a consistent definition of activities evolves.

One useful method of ensuring a consistent definition of activities is to use an activity dictionary to determine typical activities in a department. An **activity dictionary** provides a consistent starting point for defining activities by listing generic activities according to functions performed in a "typical" company within an industry. It provides a base line for defining an initial list of activities for any manufacturing environment, from smallest to largest. The generic activities are relevant to a greater or lesser extent depending on the individual company.

An activity dictionary provides a list of typical activities within a firm. It identifies the important activities that are performed by job classification within function. Each activity is presented in the form of a short statement of *what* is done (not how or why).

The activities in the dictionary are tailored to the specific company under consideration. Whether the generic activity is appropriate to the organization being studied is based on frequency of performance, cost, and time spent on each activity. Additional company-specific activities that are necessarily not part of a generic dictionary must also be defined.

A method of validating an initial definition of activities is to determine how activities are used in the decision-making process. The interview team must have a preliminary understanding of the decision-making system so that model scope, objectives, and viewpoint can be established to define activities based on typical uses of activity information.

4. *Observe activities.* The interview process should be augmented by a physical observation of the unit being analyzed to identify recurring actions (activities). The observation process is different from a detailed time-and-motion study. Observation is the nonscientific process of watching the activity being performed.

5. *Review diaries and logs.* Logging is a semiformal technique of recording what an employee does. The employee records the daily activities in a log or self-reporting diary. This method enables the analyst to gather information on the activities performed and the percentage of time spent on each. However, it requires considerable diligence on the employee's part, and many employees simply lack the skill and discipline to record their activities in clear, concise language.

6. *Consult panel of experts.* Where the department being studied is in an unstable environment or where activity analysis is being applied to newly created activities, a panel of experts can develop a consensus definition of activities based on their experience. Activity information can be obtained by assembling a group of employees from the area being analyzed or supervisors from other divisions performing similar activities to develop a consensus list of activities.

7. *Review check sheets.* A check sheet records the number of activity occurrences. It is used to gather activity data based on sample observations in order to detect patterns. Check sheets answer the question, "How often do certain events happen?" A sample check sheet follows:

Activity	Day					Total
	1	2	3	4	5	
Produce report	1 1	1		1	1 1	6
Update budget	1 1 1	1 1	1 1 1 1	1 1	1 1 1	14
Attend meeting	1 1		1		1 1	5

3c: Analyze Business Processes

The business process approach to activity definition studies the business processes that transcend organization boundaries (such as product design, materials procurement, production planning and control, and so on) and defines them in terms of major activities. The business process of procuring material, for example, is composed of activities such as the issue of purchase specifications, the selection of bid vendors, the issue of purchase orders, the receiving of parts, the storage of parts, and the payment of vendor accounts. These activities occur in a structured sequence and are interconnected by a flow of information.

A business process analysis traces inputs to outputs. Until information to perform an activity is delivered to the activity in a timely and correct manner, an activity cannot be effectively performed. The procedure is to determine the sequence of activities by following the flow of information/transaction/physical product from one activity to another. The output of one activity becomes the input to another activity. When the inputs and outputs of individual activities are connected, a business process emerges.

A flow chart is a common tool for analyzing business processes. As a pictorial representation of all the activities in a business process, it is an excellent graphic technique for examining how activities in a business process are related to one another. A flow chart uses standard symbols to represent the type of processing, as illustrated here:

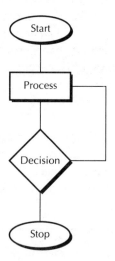

The approach is particularly applicable to continuous process manufacturing operations. Activities are defined by observing the physical flow and the change in shape or form of the product.

The advantage of this approach is that it is possible to graphically link all inputs and outputs among activities and identify interdepartmental communication routes. The disadvantage of the approach is that lateral or general activities like supervising and secretarial support may be missed. A limitation of the business process approach is that hidden processes such as general management, expediting, nonconformance, and others may not be identified and included in the analysis.

A business process analysis usually results in a revision of the initial activity definition developed by interviews. Organizational units might aggregate activities that are an important part of a business process. Often key activities, inputs, or outputs are missing. This results in disconnected business processes. The activity gaps require a reanalysis of the impacted activities.

The final output of a business process analysis is a set of diagrams or views that represent the interrelationship of activities and their information flows. An important tool used to define business processes is the PERT chart, which portrays the relationship between activities and their timing.

3d: Analyze Business Functions

The functional approach to activity definition breaks down each major function (such as quality or security) into activities. For example, the function of purchasing may be broken down into activities such as finding suitable suppliers, negotiating prices, agreeing on quality standards, and maintaining records. This approach allows common activities (such as secretarial services) to be considered across the whole business. It treats common problems as part of a single analysis.

The description of a function should as precisely as possible answer the question, "What does it do?" The description should contain a verb and noun only. The verb should be active and should have a direct object. The noun should be measurable. For example, the function of overhauling a tank engine could be defined as "maintain engine." The overhaul of the engine is a specific activity that is a subset of the maintenance function. The maintenance is performed for the engine, a major item.

An example of a functional activity analysis is on the following page.

There are two primary methods for reporting functional activities. The first is to treat them separately from the organizations performing the activity—that is, count them only once. The second method is to include the activity in the organization performing the activity and report it as a "ghost" function. This means that each department analyzed has, for example, its secretaries included in its total cost. However, the activities can be summarized across the whole business—that is, in more than one format.

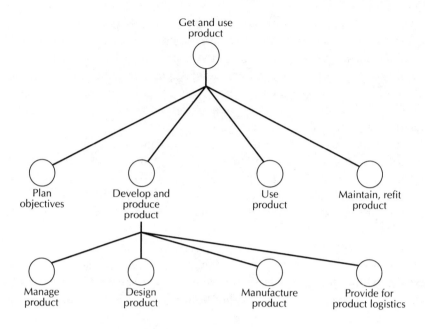

3e: Conduct Directed Industrial Engineering Study

An industrial engineering study is a precise but expensive method of defining activities. In this approach an industrial engineering team uses standard work analysis techniques such as timed observation to assess an organization's significant activities.

An important engineering method is timed observation. This is a method of gathering activity information by watching employees perform their daily activities. It is particularly appropriate for factory or clerical jobs that are repetitive, are of short duration, and have observable work cycles. If some elements of the job occur at infrequent or irregular intervals, observation is not practical. Managerial and administration jobs are not suitable to this approach.

3f: Reconcile Activity Definition

Although all the activity definition approaches have different starting points, they are merely different methods of defining the same set of activities and therefore require reconciliation. For example, the business process of procuring material consists of activities that are a subset of various organizational units involved in the material procurement process.

When choosing an approach, one must define the desired purpose of the analysis. For example, a functional analysis is rarely appropriate for analyzing a possible restructuring of a business. Only when the relationship between various departments is determined can alternative organization structures be suggested.

Additionally, it is important to make use of existing information. For example, an activity analysis might have been previously used as part of a process improvement, system design, factory modernization, or zero-base budgeting project. It is prudent to use the existing information and then to supplement it with further activity analysis.

It is advisable to begin an activity analysis with an organizational review of each department followed by a business process or functional analysis. The activity definition is completed after the subsequent analysis. The secondary activity definition techniques are used to fine-tune or reconcile the activity definition.

STEP 4: RATIONALIZE ACTIVITIES

The key to meaningful activity definition is to structure an activity list that provides a sufficient but not excessive level of detail. The more simplified the activity list, the easier it is to manage and positively influence business decisions. A detailed activity analysis invalidates many of the benefits of an activity accounting system. Such systems are complex and not focused on key decision variables. They therefore tend to be expensive and ineffective.

However, an excessively simple system does not provide the level of detail necessary to properly account for activity cost behavior. The degree of simplification is influenced to an extent by the complexity of the business, but it is far more likely to be affected by the type of industry and the type of customer. Separating activities with different cost behavior patterns results in more accurate product costing and improved decision making. The cost of measurement will be higher, however, because two sets of measurements must be made.

Often the flows between activities within a business process provide insight into how to decompose activities. A flow of information or outputs delineates activities. When a business process analysis identifies a new information flow that can not be accounted for by previously defined activities, the activity should be decomposed. Similarly, when a business process analysis identifies no flow of information between two previously defined activities, the activity should be aggregated.

Although the activity accounting system requires tasks to be aggregated into activities, performance improvement requires an activity to be broken down into tasks, operations, and elements. Activities are too global to identify where changes should be implemented to improve activity performance; only work elements can be modified.

For zero-base budgeting, for example, it is important to break down an individual's time typically to a minimum of 10 hours per month. A **work measurement** system would work in terms of standard time units (STU), which are 0.00001 hours (30 STUs equate to approximately one second). For example, 72 STUs are allowed for picking up, holding, and putting down a pen.

Rationalization Criteria

Aggregation of activities with very different economics is best avoided. For example, it would be desirable to keep advertising and promotion separate since the relevant cost driver for advertising is total company market share, whereas promotional costs are often specific to a product or product line.

One must guard against aggregating dissimilar activities. Otherwise a single activity measure will inaccurately reflect the cost behavior pattern. As a consequence, a product cost based on the amount the product consumes of each activity is not a valid indicator of the total resources apportioned to the activity. An invalid activity measure makes it impossible to predict and manage the correct amount of resources necessary to produce a given amount of output.

For example, when the activities of designing a new product are combined with those of configuration control, the cost behavior patterns are significantly different. The design engineering cost for new products benefits the product over its entire life cycle and should be capitalized. The engineering costs associated with configuration control benefit only a specific order and should be directly charged to that order. Two separate and distinct activities should be established.

The most common problem facing the activity analysis team is not decomposing activities but aggregating them. It is human nature for people to explain what they do at a significant level of detail; that is, they articulate their tasks. All the individual tasks necessary to perform an activity should be combined and treated as part of a single activity.

To summarize/decompose activities, one must break down each major activity to the level of detail where costs are proportionately distributed among activities with homogeneous inputs and outputs. The magnitude of the activity are based on estimates of time and resources apportioned to each activity. The process requires a balance of costs at a level of detail that is fine enough to be manageable but not so fine that it becomes complex and expensive to operate. It is tempting to decompose an activity too far. You can apply several tests to determine whether an activity has been decomposed to a low enough level:

- If an activity is part of a decision-making process, then it is an ideal candidate for decomposition. The decision scope and objectives aid in determining which activities to decompose.
- If knowing the cost and performance of an activity would not make any difference to the decision model, then the activity probably should not be decomposed any further.
- If an activity corresponds directly to a repetitive action in the enterprise that is already at its lowest level, then the activity should not be decomposed further.
- If an activity cannot be modified, then it is of little value to decompose it further.
- If at least one input and one output for each activity cannot be defined, then the definition of the activity must be refined.
- If there are multiple *primary* outputs from an activity, the activity should be decomposed into a number of different activities. It is permissible to have by-products.
- If an activity cannot be associated with a business process, an alternative activity definition should be sought.
- If the inputs and outputs of an activity are identical, then there is a strong possibility that they are tasks and part of the same activity. For example, say two activities identified by the accounts receivable department were:
  - Check customer credit
  - Approve/disapprove customer credit

  Both supposed activities were triggered by a customer order, processed by the same person, and the output was an approval or rejection. Therefore, they are tasks rather than activities.
- If an activity has multiple inputs and outputs, then it should be decomposed into different activities.
- The activity must add value to be of benefit to an organization.
- The activity should always be something that could be subcontracted to a separate company.

STEP 5: CLASSIFY AS PRIMARY OR SECONDARY

Each activity should be classified as primary or secondary. A primary activity is one whose output is used outside an organizational unit. Activities used within a department to support the primary activities are secondary activities. Activity classification is necessary to apportion the cost of secondary activities to the primary activities and to manage the ratio of secondary activities to primary activities.

STEP 6: CREATE ACTIVITY MAP

An activity map identifies the relationship between functions, business processes, and activities. Creating an activity map is the first step in analyzing alternative business processes and activities to perform a function. Activity accounting maps the company's activities and describes the cost structure in terms of activity consumption. An example of an activity map follows:

Activity Map

Function	Alternatives		
Product development	Patent acquisition	License	Internal development
Material procurement	Process recovery	Purchase	Trade
Quality assurance	System		Component
Material preparation	Pickling		Kiln dry
Form	Lathe / Mill		Plane / Forge
Paint	Prime		
	Manual	Electrostatic	
Quality control	Test		
Rework		Scrap	Rework
Package	Shrink wrap		Box
Store/ship	Direct ship	Warehouse / Distribute	
Sell	Advertise, market, and sell		

After business processes and activities have been mapped to functions, the next step is to map activities to business processes. This step is illustrated in the following chart:

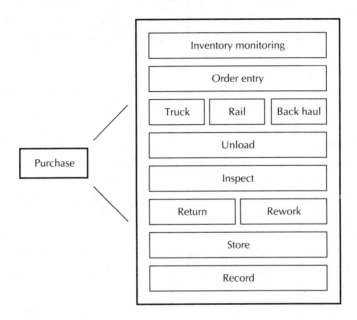

STEP 7: FINALIZE AND DOCUMENT ACTIVITIES

The final step is to compile a composite list of activities that support the organizational, business process, and functional analysis requirements.

SUMMARY

As companies begin to move from cost accounting to cost management, the importance of implementing an activity accounting system becomes paramount. Activities provide valuable insight into what causes costs so that management can take the initiative to eliminate or minimize these costs.

6

ACTIVITIES OF AN INDUSTRIAL ENTERPRISE

The purpose of this chapter is to:

- Define the functions in an industrial organization. A consistent and comprehensive activity definition is essential to ensure an effective activity accounting system that permits comparison of divisions and companies.
- Serve as a basis for introducing changes to activities to facilitate cost reduction and performance improvement. Today, special attention to such problems, through the creation of specific functions, is justified more than ever before.

In order to exist, any enterprise, regardless of size, must perform certain essential functions. An individual employee in a small business might perform numerous activities, or the company might contract them to outside professionals. Large corporations, on the other hand, require hundreds or even thousands of employees to support all the needed functions.

All the different activities of a business must be coordinated to operate effectively; this requires organization. The business organization structure is the means by which an enterprise coordinates the activities of different elements—human energy, physical assets, time, and money—to achieve corporate objectives. Organization is the grouping of activities to facilitate the flow of information, accomplishment of work, and control. The groupings vary from business to business and enterprise to enterprise, but they always include the basic functions described in this chapter.

Traditionally, there are five major groupings of functions in an industrial enterprise:

1. Marketing and sales
2. Manufacturing and quality control
3. Research and development and engineering

4. Finance and administration

5. Field support and logistics

MARKETING AND SALES

The marketing and sales function appears in business organizations in different forms. An enterprise may have a single marketing function that includes marketing or sales, or it may have two separate departments. The mission of the marketing function is to direct the flow of goods and services from the producer to the user.

In simple terms the *marketing* function determines the consumer or user needs and informs the market of the organization's products. The *sales* function consummates the transaction. It tells manufacturing what to manufacture and when and where to ship and provides the necessary customer service to resolve any problems with the product.

Various types of marketing organizational structures exist. Many marketing departments are organized by product lines. Others are organized geographically so that a given department is charged with marketing in a specific region. Still others are organized by major customer accounts. These different groupings do not in any way change the basic mission nor the activities performed. They merely change the assignment of responsibility for performing the activity.

Marketing determines the demand for existing products and identifies the need for new products. This is done by the **market research** subfunction. The market research group evaluates market needs and translates them into requirements such as the features required for a given product. Market research reexamines the product's intended and actual uses, identifies the features or specifications for the perceived demand, and verifies those that are absolutely essential to the marketability of the product.

A second mission of marketing is to communicate to potential buyers what products or services the business has to offer and at what price. Advertising and promotional activities are key communication activities. Through such efforts market share can be maintained or expanded.

Still another marketing activity is to forecast and plan the number of units of products to be manufactured to support demand. Costs and projections of units of sales are closely intertwined.

Finally, the marketing function processes orders, handles requests for product literature, maintains a distribution network, and schedules delivery dates.

The main activities in the marketing function include the following:

Activity	Decision
Product/product line specification	Number of variations New product introduction Product abandonment Product modification
Providing customer service	Range of guarantees Pricing for service activities
Developing distribution channels	Number of distribution channels Types of distribution channels
Completing finished goods inventory	Inventory level
Product shipping	Shipping channel
Determining discount policy	Discount policy
Product pricing	Product variation Special orders
Sales promotion	Type of promotion
Order processing	Processing sales orders
Product sale	Selling products to customers

MANUFACTURING AND QUALITY CONTROL

The manufacturing function involves procuring necessary materials, transforming materials into finished goods, and shipping the finished product to customers. The quality control function ensures that all materials entering the plant and all finished goods leaving it conform to predetermined specifications.

The manufacturing function consists of direct production activities that can be organized in different ways, depending on factors such as volume of production, diversity of operations, single or multiplant operations, proximity of the plants, and so on.

Factory Operations

The **materials management** function regulates the movement of raw materials, supplies, and finished goods through the plant. The key materials management activities include:

- Production control
- Coordination of change
- Receiving and shipping

- Materials and supplies procurement
- Inventory control

Production control informs the manufacturing operations what equipment is needed to make a given part. It plans the sequence of operations and determines economic lot quantities. Production control checks inventory availability and triggers the procurement of materials and supplies. It plans the dates when finished parts will arrive at the stockroom or warehouse and be available for shipping.

Receiving and shipping are the two points within the plant through which all goods pass, both when entering the factory and when leaving it.

The procurement function, often called purchasing, involves the purchase, receipt, inspection, and storage of raw materials. It plays an important role in selecting vendors and subcontractors and in negotiating prices and lead times. Purchasing notifies production control of the lead times, and production control, in turn, uses them to plan production schedules.

The inventory control group determines how much or how many of a product or material is on hand and where it is stored.

The manufacturing engineering subgroup includes the following activities:

- Industrial engineering
- Production engineering
- Plant engineering
- Machine design

Industrial engineering determines the labor content of the manufacturing processes and specifies the best manufacturing methods. It conducts time-and-motion studies and develops production standards. Production engineering decides how much of the part or assembly can be made in-house and what needs to be subcontracted. It determines what processes and machines to utilize and what kinds of tools and fixtures are needed. The machine design section designs any special machinery, tooling, and fixtures. Plant engineering, or facilities, assigns floor space to specified activities. It is responsible for the design of electrical, air, oil, or similar hook-ups, and chip removal. Plant engineering often includes building and grounds maintenance.

The quality control function is charged with ensuring that all products leaving the factory conform to predetermined marketing and customer specifications. Incoming inspection and vendor control ensure that all incoming raw material and purchased subassemblies conform to engineering specifications. Quality control also monitors all factory activities to make sure that they consistently produce acceptable parts and assemblies. It provides the necessary measuring instruments, gauges, and calibration and determines the in-process inspection points. It is responsible for final product testing.

Finally, the factory operation function is responsible for manufacturing. Here the parts are fabricated and assembled and finished products are packed and shipped. Design errors, poor estimates, and wrong assumptions eventually surface in the shop.

The main activities of a manufacturing and quality control function include the following:

Activity	Decision
Materials management	
Production planning	Equipment scheduling
Coordination of change	Operation sequencing
Receiving	Determination of economic lot quantities
Production control	Inventory checking
Routing	Requesting materials and supplies
Scheduling	Scheduling material receipts
Inventory control	Managing physical inventory and inventory records
Material and supplies procurement	
Plan procurement	Analyzing material specs
	Value engineering
Vendor selection and evaluation	Selecting vendor
	Assessing vendor
Negotiation of price, delivery, and quality	Negotiating with vendor
	Quality control of vendor
Purchase order completion	PO issue
	PO tracking
	PO receipt
Vendor coordination	Vendor coordination
	Expediting
Distribution	
Finished goods management	Controlling finished manufactured part
Transportation/shipping	Selecting method of transportation to customer
Packaging	Packaging finished goods

Field support — Maintaining product at customer location

Spares management — Providing spares
Equipment maintenance — Maintaining distribution equipment

Dealerships — Selecting dealerships

Manufacturing engineering
  Industrial engineering: — Specifying labor content
    Determining time standards — Determining best methods
    Method selection
    Investment justification — Evaluating and selecting capital equipment

    Completing special projects
    Prepare customer quotations/proposals
  Production engineering
    Make/buy analysis — Subcontracting
    Process planning — Routing
      Machine and process selection
      Tool and fixture selection

Plant engineering
  Plant and office layout — Allocating floor space
    Designing plant

  Environmental control
  Grounds and building maintenance
  Equipment set-up — Lot size

Machine design
  Tool, fixture, and equipment design
  Tool room design

Quality control
  Quality specification — Determining that parts meet specification

  Incoming inspection — Controlling quality of incoming material

  In-process inspection — Establishing in-process inspection points

  Final inspection — Controlling quality of final product

  Tool and gauge control — Controlling quality of tools and gauges

  Maintenance and operation of inspection equipment — Setting maintenance policy
  Evaluation of vendor quality and qualification — Selecting vendor

  Product certification — Determining cost and time to obtain product certification

RESEARCH AND DEVELOPMENT AND ENGINEERING

The research and development (R&D) function develops new ideas for products and materials. The engineering function designs new products and modifies existing ones. Research and development and engineering provide the link between marketing and manufacturing. The needs of the marketplace are used to determine the direction of research and the products to be manufactured. Customer wants, as perceived by marketing, are translated into the designs, part numbers, bills of materials, drawings, and specifications used by manufacturing to make the products.

The R&D function is expected to stay at the cutting edge of technologies relevant to a company's business. In particular it is expected to maintain the capability of solving special technical problems and to actively participate in the initial phase of new product development. During that phase it must prove out a new product concept and develop broad guidelines for engineering—all within market-determined cost and performance targets.

R&D includes the following activities:

- Basic research
- Applied research

The product engineering function translates product specifications into a product design. It continues to develop and refine the design until it falls within the limits of cost, performance, and producibility. Finally, it puts all that information into engineering reports, specification sheets, bills of materials, and drawings.

The testing laboratory is set up to support the theoretical activities of research and engineering. The degree of sophistication of the laboratory may vary with the nature and complexity of company products, but it is always an inseparable part of the research and development cycle. Laboratory personnel usually design and build the test fixtures, perform the testing, and collect test data. They assist with the design of the tests, selection of instrumentation, and interpretation of test results. The laboratory often has a model shop where fixtures and prototype hardware are built.

The technical administration function is an administrative and service function within research and engineering. It includes the complete spectrum of drafting services where all the necessary drawings are developed and maintained, bills of materials are structured, and part numbers are issued. Original drawings, original bills of materials, product structure records, and final test reports are maintained and distributed to all who need them.

The technical administration group manages the development and maintenance of research software and computer hardware and maintains the technical library.

The engineering function includes the following activities:

- New product engineering
- Engineering changes
- Laboratory testing
- Technical administration

The main activities of a research and development and engineering function include:

Activity	Decision
New product development	When to introduce new products Pricing
Existing product modification	Number of products Number of product modifications Pricing
Basic research	New product requirement Pricing
R&D processing	New processes requirement Pricing

FINANCE AND ADMINISTRATION

The finance and administration function gathers and processes financial and performance data. The finance function provides the financial planning required to manage the cash flow to meet company financial obligations. Loan payments, dividend payments, and disbursements for goods and services purchased are coordinated by the finance department. The financial function issues all recurring financial reports; manages payroll, accounts payable, and accounts receivable; and prepares profit plans. It administers the budget and provides guidelines and assistance during the budget cycle.

An important subfunction of finance is cost accounting. Cost accounting compiles the production expenses and maintains product cost data.

The **management information system (MIS)** is responsible for acquiring and maintaining the central computer and peripheral equipment and for developing and maintaining the software programs used to support the computer facility and the application programs. The computer is usually used to process data within the management information system, which can include such items as analysis of quality deviations or headcount and skills bank, or it might even be used to run the entire material requirement plan (MRP), starting with the sales forecast and the master schedule and ending with work or machine center loading.

The finance and administration group often includes the function of labor relations and personnel management. It is responsible for items like personnel recruitment, employee training, performance appraisal administration, compensation management, employee counseling, vacations, health plan administration, and so forth. It also provides assistance in labor contract negotiations and administration.

The main activities of a finance and administration function include the following:

Activity

Accounting and finance

Cost accounting
  Data acquisition/maintenance
  General reporting
  Government reporting

Accounts payable
  Requisitioning
  Invoice receipt
  Payments
  Cash management

Accounts receivable
  Issue of invoices and credit memos
  Credit checks and maintenance
  Receiving/processing remittance
  Cash management

Payroll
  Maintenance and collection of employee data
  Issue of checks

General ledger
  Monthly closing
  Budgeting
  External reporting
  Internal control

Corporate management
Legal decisions
Public relations
Executive staffing
Treasury/tax decisions
Stockholder relations
Strategic planning
Insurance decisions
Pension administration

Management information systems, development, operation, and maintenance

Operations
  Hardware
  Operating systems
  Security
  Operating expenses:
    Personnel
    Power

Applications
  Software:
    MRP
    BOM
    AP/AR
  Database:
    MRP
    BOM
    AP/AR

General and administrative management
General management
Division management
Senior management
Product, program management

Personnel
Reporting
Maintenance of employee data
Administration of benefits
Training
Union contract negotiation and administration
Recruiting
Retirement

LOGISTICS AND FIELD SUPPORT

Customer service is a subfunction of marketing that resolves product problems after shipment to the customer. The activities associated with customer service resulting from product problems are non–value added because they result only from manufacturing problems. The costs are significant where there is warranty cost, defect cost, repair cost, and cost of sales in addition to the cost of the customer service department. The redesign of a product that is introduced along with cost-reducing changes simultaneously reduces warranty cost.

Second, field testing is normally a customer service activity. A network of field service representatives conducts field tests of pilot production. In many instances, when product changes are extensive or laboratory testing cannot determine the reliability of a new design, field testing under actual user conditions is absolutely mandatory.

SUMMARY

In order to exist, all organizations must perform certain basic business functions. Each function has a specific mission around which activities are structured. The manner in which organizations accomplish their activities (tasks) to achieve their mission will vary dramatically among companies, but there is a degree of commonality at the activity level. Tasks differ dramatically between different companies as they seek to maximize the efficiency of flow of information and the accomplishment of the activities.

Developing an understanding of the typical activities in an industrial enterprise provides an excellent foundation for structuring an activity accounting system.

7

ACTIVITY COST

The purpose of this chapter is to:

- Describe how to calculate an activity cost
- Explain the role of variable and fixed costs in the decision-making process
- Describe how activity cost is used in the decision-making process
- Describe how to select an activity measure
- Identify important activity cost considerations
- Describe an activity measure and distinguish it from a cost driver
- Discuss how activity measures are used to influence behavior

An activity cost is the total expense of all traceable factors of production assigned to perform an activity. Costs are considered *traceable* when the output of an activity can be shown to be directly consumed by another activity or end cost objective. A cost is *allocated* when it is charged to another activity or cost objective on a basis other than direct traceability. The rationale for allocating costs is to ensure that business decisions include *all* costs.

Activity cost is expressed in terms of an activity measure by which the cost of a given process varies most directly. Examples of activity measures include machine hours, number of inserts, manhours, and number of payroll checks. The activity volume represents the number of occurrences of the activity. Finally, activity costs are traced to cost objectives such as products, processes, and orders on the basis of usage of the activity.

An activity is a homogeneous grouping of cost because resources are assigned to produce a specific output. *Homogeneity* means that variation in an activity is explained by a single activity measure. For example, the activity of manually processing a payroll check is homogeneous since the number of payroll checks (activity measure) dictates the level of resources applied to the activity. As long as the output or method of performing the activity is not changed, the necessary resources will vary in proportion to the activity measure. Thus **homogeneous cost** is a cost in which each activity has a similar cause-and-effect relationship to the cost objective.

The conventional approach of capturing costs at the cost element level aggregates multiple demands for a factor of production. To know the total travel expenses of a department, for example, does not provide any insight into the activities that generate the need for travel. To control travel cost one must first understand the factors (such as activities) that drive the need for travel.

The conventional approach to cost accounting considers only the total cost of an activity without regard to its output. Measuring activity effectiveness requires knowing the amount of output (activity volume) as well as the factors of production assigned to an activity. The selection of the activity measure is critical since it makes visible the factors that influence activity volume and subsequently cost. The factor also allows management to perform "what if" analysis.

Expressing the cost of activities by unit of output provides a means to accurately trace costs to products, manufacturing processes, customers, or other cost objectives. To properly trace costs to products, one must determine how much of each activity is consumed in the product. Consider a complex product that requires an average of 20 purchase orders, as opposed to a simple product that requires 1 purchase order. An accurate product cost is possible only when the complex product absorbs a greater proportion of the purchase order activity than the simple product.

Knowing the cost per activity is also important in managing cost. The cost per activity output is a *productivity* measure. To judge the effectiveness of the purchase order activity, one must know the number of purchase orders processed. For example, the current cost to process 6,000 purchase orders is $120,000 or $20 per purchase order. If, as the result of improvements in the purchasing department, the company is able to process 10,000 purchase orders for the same cost, the new cost per purchase order would be reduced to $12.

Knowing the cost per activity is important because it facilitates a comparison of the cost of processing purchase orders within different divisions in order to identify the most cost-effective operation. The most proficient operation can then be studied to specify a set of best practices that aid other organizations in improving work methods. For this reason, activity cost is expressed as a measure of activity volume by which the costs of a given process vary most directly.

ACTIVITY COST BEHAVIOR PATTERNS*

An activity's cost behavior pattern is defined as the variation of an activity cost with changes in activity volume. It is used to predict the level of resources (cost) necessary to support a given level of activity volume. In other words, there is a close bond between an activity's cost and the number of its occurrences.

An activity cost is the cost of all traceable factors of production divided by planned activity volume. A standard (planned) activity cost is the sum of the cost of traceable factors of production at a planned activity volume. Thus an activity's standard cost depends on a forecast of the number of activity occurrences.

The cost behavior pattern has no impact on the ability to establish a cause-and-effect relationship. The cost behavior pattern is related to the varability of cost with production volume. In other words, traceability is related to cause-and-effect, but the cost behavior pattern is related to a fixed/variable distinction.

An activity's cost behavior depends on several attributes of the factors of production assigned to the activity. It is a function of the capacity of the factors of production and their flexibility to alternative uses. The primary attributes include the following:

- Fixedness/variability
- Influenceability
- Flexibility

Fixedness Versus Variability

A **variable cost** changes in proportion to production volume in the short term. (All costs are variable in the long run.) A **fixed cost** does not vary with production volume in the short run. For example, a laborer's cost per hour is assumed to be constant, but total labor cost varies with production volume (a variable cost). A robot's cost per hour varies with production volume, but the total cost is the same regardless of production volume (a fixed cost).

---

*Acknowledgment: Much of this section is based on input from William Sullivan of the Virginia Polytechnic Institute.

To illustrate the difference between fixed and variable cost, consider the process of inserting components into electronic boards. A manual insertion process employs laborers as the primary factor of production. The technology is unsophisticated—bins of components. In this environment, there is a relatively direct relationship between the number of laborers and production volume since laborers are generally flexible and can perform other activities.

Variable costs tend to rise or fall directly in proportion to business volume. They are controllable in the short term. Traceable variable costs include the following:

- People-related costs
- Material costs
- Royalties
- **Overtime premiums**

For people-related costs, an hourly rate is computed by dividing the employee rate by the available hours. A product would absorb the laborers' cost based on the number of hours consumed by the product multiplied by their hourly rate. Unused hours are treated as an efficiency variance.

Technology costs are treated differently. The cost of a machine is considered depreciation, which is included in overhead and is allocated to products. For example, an automated insertion process would employ machines as the primary factor of production. Machine operators, maintenance personnel, NC programmers, and others would be important but secondary factors of production that support the automated processes. There is a stepped relationship between the technology costs and production volume. Additional production volume, where unutilized capacity exists, can be absorbed without the need to incur additional cost until full capacity is reached. Also, technology is often inflexible, and the machines are not easily changed for alternative uses.

A fixed cost has two components—actual capacity used and unused capacity. Whereas the total costs of a machine are relative of actual volume usage, the treatment of unused capacity has a dramatic impact on cost. An activity rate based on actual or forecasted capacity charges unused capacity to current period products. An activity rate based on practical capacity, on the other hand, charges current production costs only with the cost of actual capacity used. The cost of unused capacity is transferred to a management account and classified as a **non–value added cost**. To illustrate the difference between the two approaches, consider a machine that cost $100,000 with an actual usage of 7,500 machine hours and a practical capacity of 10,000 machine hours.

Method 1—Cost based on actual usage:

$$\frac{\text{Cost}}{\text{Actual Usage}} = \frac{\$100,000}{7,500} = \$15/\text{machine hour}$$

Method 2—Cost based on theoretical usage:

$$\frac{\text{Cost}}{\text{Practical capacity}} = \frac{\$100,000}{10,000} = \$10/\text{machine hour}$$

$$\frac{\text{Unused capacity}}{\text{cost}} = \frac{\text{Practical capacity less actual usage} \times \text{cost}}{\text{Practical capacity}}$$

$$= \frac{(10,000 - 7,500) \times \$100,000}{10,000}$$

$$= \$5/\text{machine hour}$$

The accounting treatment of fixed cost is a direct consequence of the accountant's view of depreciation. Companies purchase assets with the expectation of using them to generate revenue. An expense is associated with generating this revenue, since using the asset causes it to deteriorate. For a proper statement of net income, the revenue generated by an asset must be matched with the corresponding expense of using it. Depreciation is the accounting mechanism used to provide this match. Depreciation takes the historical cost of an asset and systematically allocates it in proportion to the contribution it is expected to make in the generation of profit each period. It is important to note that the accountant's motivation for depreciation is the proper determination of net income. This income adjustment appears on the balance sheet as accumulated depreciation and acts as a liability against the equipment asset account.

To properly assign a robot or other fixed cost requires a reasonable forecast of future production volume. Whether the manufacturing company produces one unit or one million units, the cost of the machine must be absorbed.

In addition to depreciable assets, other resources are often considered *fixed*. They are largely related to the support of the ongoing enterprise, the so-called overhead of management, accounting, finance and advertising, sales, R&D, and market development. All tend to build up as business grows and are controllable in the long term. The primary costs include the following:

- Property taxes
- Rent
- Cleaning
- Maintenance of building
- Insurance
- Executive salaries
- Auditing expense

Other *shared (nontraceable)* costs are like a franchise fee. These include all the other costs incurred to support the business that are not readily traceable to any activity. They are included in overhead of the corporation, division, or plant as well as SG&A (selling, general, and administrative) expense.

The distinction between fixed and variable cost has been considered of permanent importance since it determines whether a cost changes in a step-wise or linear relationship to volume.

Influenceability

Managers have significant influence over the efficiency and effectiveness of the activities in their area of responsibility. Managers control how activities are accomplished and select or influence the factors of production to perform an activity. An *influenceable* activity is one that can be changed by the business in the short term. The degree of influenceability varies according to timing and company policy.

Not all activities can be changed in the short term. Factors of production such as machines, equipment, and information systems are normally changed only in the medium to short term. However, they are traceable to the activity and therefore are controllable.

Certain activities are influenced by external factors such as regulations and weather. However, even these factors are somewhat influenceable in the long run.

Flexibility

The *flexibility* of an activity is the degree to which its factors of production are adaptable to alternative uses. The greater the degree of flexibility, the more linear the relationship between cost and production volume. Conversely, the lesser the flexibility, the more stepwise the relationship between cost and production volume.

ACTIVITY COST IN DECISION MAKING

An activity's cost behavior has traditionally been an important factor in decision making. Proponents of classical contribution analysis hold that separating fixed cost from variable cost is important because a business decision that leads to the recovery of all the variable costs and at least a portion of the fixed costs improves the company's financial position.

Fixed costs are considered **sunk costs**. The argument is that nothing can be done to influence sunk costs, so they are irrelevant to future decisions. The concept of whether to exclude sunk cost, long-term influenceable costs, from short-term decisions has been the subject of great controversy over the years. One problem associated with sunk cost is there is no single, consistently used definition for the term. Often the struggle over the concept of sunk cost arises because two very different ideas are being discussed under the same title.

In the context of management decision making, sunk cost has two distinct meanings. First, it corresponds to the accounting definition of book value minus salvage value. In this context a sunk cost is the unallocated portion of the equipment's historical cost. Depreciation is an estimated value that seeks to allocate the expense of using the equipment over its useful life. This goal is not always attainable due to factors such as obsolescence, product changes, and capacity shifts. The result is that equipment is retired before the end of its initially estimated life. Because the equipment did not generate revenue over the period estimated, some of the retired equipment's historical cost remains unmatched to a revenue-generating period. This unallocated amount is called **book value**. The book value minus any proceeds from the sale of the retired asset is called *loss on disposal* or *sunk cost*. In the accountant's mind it is a sunk cost because it is lost. Part of the asset's cost was never recovered by revenue generation, so this lost cost must be recovered from other sources like capital accumulation account. For example, suppose a numerical control milling machine was purchased for $50,000 and depreciated over four years using straight line depreciation. After three years the machine is scrapped (zero salvage value) and a new one bought. The balance sheet would appear as follows:

NC milling machine	$50,000
Less accumulated depreciation	($37,500)
	$12,500

The accountant views the asset as an unallocated historical cost of $12,500. The unallocated cost must be recovered from somewhere—it can't be ignored. The account must be reconciled. The reconciliation is accomplished by claiming a loss on disposal or sunk cost. So to the accountant a sunk cost is an accounting balance equal to book value minus salvage value.

Many accountants are reluctant to trace fixed costs or allocate them to specific products because of the mistaken view that they are not short-term controllable and should not impact short-term decisions. Also, it is impossible to allocate nontraceable costs with the perceived degree of precision that accounting professionals normally use to develop traditional financial statements. There is a natural aversion to allocating in an imprecise manner. There is simply no way, however, to know how well or badly a product is doing without tracing these costs.

Second, sunk cost is viewed as any cost made in the past or any cost that will not affect the decision at hand. The central theme is relevance. Since past costs are viewed as nonrecoverable and unalterable, they are sunk. They are irrelevant to the current decision. So while the accountant views sunk cost as an accounting balance that must always be recovered, decision makers generally view it as an unalterable past expenditure.

An important issue in activity accounting is whether sunk costs are relevant in future-directed decisions. Horngren, in a book on managerial cost accounting, speaks strongly against using sunk cost.* He states, "The term sunk cost should not be used at all. It muddles the task of collecting proper costs for decision making. Because all past costs are irrelevant, it is fruitless to introduce unnecessary terms to describe past costs." From an engineering economy point of view, Canada and Sullivan express a similar view when they state, "Sunk costs are costs resulting from past decisions or commitments and . . . are therefore irrelevant to the consideration of alternative courses of action." The common theme is that because sunk costs will remain constant for all decisions, they must not be considered relevant.

Proponents of direct traceability, on the other hand, hold that the prime factor in routine decisions is whether the cost is traceable. A routine decision is one for which the current planning assumptions are valid. Managers must, therefore, treat all assets as an investment and obtain a fair return on the investment.

Under the concept of direct traceability, the primary factor in a routine decision is whether a cause-and-effect relationship can be established be-

---

*Charles T. Horngren and George Foster, *Cost Accounting, A Managerial Emphasis,* 6th ed. (1987), Prentice Hall, Englewood Cliffs, N. J., p. 326.

tween an activity and the product. Where direct traceability is established, the cost is relevant to the business decision. The concept is based on the observation that for routine decisions all resources represent investments, and management should recover all costs associated with the investment.

Consider a manufacturing process of inserting electronic components in a PC board. When the process is performed by a human, the salary cost would be considered a variable cost and included in the decisions based on the amount of labor. If the human were replaced with a robot, the product would remain identical. However, from a contribution analysis decision perspective the cost would be considered a fixed sunk cost and excluded from the decision process.

A key difference between contribution analysis and direct traceability is the treatment of future alternatives. Advocates of direct traceability maintain that the assumptions made during the planning phase are valid and management has a responsibility to sell products or services that return at least the cost of the investment. Advocates of contribution analysis assume that all future alternatives are known and a company would choose a mix of products that contributes the most to covering the fixed cost.

There are several fallacies involved in the use of contribution analysis for routine decisions. First, a consequence of contribution analysis is that the company's portfolio of products is a mixture of profitable products that subsidize the fixed costs of other products. The resulting cross-subsidization increases the vulnerability of a company to competitive pressures. Other companies are most likely to compete for the most profitable products since their products are not burdened by subsidizing the fixed cost of other products. As companies lose market share, the impact on profit margins for the most profitable products is devastating because the profit margins decrease at a faster rate than the loss of sales for products being subsidized.

A second impact of selling a product that does not cover all traceable costs is that it sets a market expectation. Once a customer becomes accustomed to a certain price level, it is more difficult to raise than to lower prices.

A well-managed company will strive to offer a mix of self-sufficient products and manage all internal investments to ensure that returns forecasted during the planning stage are realized. It is easy to forgo managerial excellence and make decisions that appear to help the short-term performance but increase the long-term vulnerability of a company.

Costs in the traceable category are controllable—in either the long or short term. Generally, as a business expands, costs tend to be far more variable than they should be, and when it contracts, they are far more fixed than they should be.

A bill of activities does not require a distinction between volume-related or non–volume-related costs. Both are traced according to actual usage rather than allocated.

ESTABLISHING A CAUSAL RELATIONSHIP

When a cause-and-effect relationship can be established between a factor of production and a specific activity, the cost is said to be *traceable*. In many cases, tracing an activity is reasonably simple because the resource is dedicated to a single activity. An accounts payable clerk, for example, can be easily traced to the accounts payable activity. When a resource supports several activities, the resource usage must be split among them. For example, in a small company a clerk may perform accounts payable, accounts receivable, financial statement preparation, and payroll activities.

A causal relationship exists when a factor of production can be shown to be directly consumed by an activity. Assume a clerk spends 15 minutes processing a work order. A causal relationship between the cost of the clerk and the activity of processing work orders has been established. It is an indisputable fact that the clerk spent 15 minutes processing the work order. Therefore, the cost of the clerk is traceable to the work order processing activity.

Typical causal bases include:

Factor of Production	Measure
People	Time
Technology	Machine/technology hours
Facilities	Square footage
Utilities	Kilowatt hours

ACTIVITY COST CONSIDERATIONS

The cost of an activity includes all the factors of production employed to perform an activity. The factors of production consist of people, machines, travel, supplies, computer systems, and other resources that are customarily expressed as cost elements within a chart of accounts. Each significant factor of production is included in cost. For instance, the activity of scheduling production requires a person to make the scheduling decision and a computer system to perform the necessary calculations and data manipulation. Other resources such as office supplies are required. The cost of the activity is determined by tracing the labor, technology, and office supplies to the scheduling activity. A causal relationship has been established between the factors of production and the scheduling activity.

An intercompany activity supports activities in other departments. It is a resource (cost) that is consumed along with the natural factors of production. Important characteristics of intercompany activities are (1) their support for other company activities (2) their importance to the using activity, and (3) their ability to be located there. The using department support activities are often centralized to achieve economies of scale.

When costs are not traceable to activities, they are allocated on a basis such as percentage of time, units of production, or historical data. The assumptions on which allocations are based should be documented and tested for reasonableness. The activity accounting system must be able to support the choice of assumptions by making clear exactly what is being costed, where the factors came from (for instance, general ledger and statistical data derived from regression analysis), and how the results were calculated.

ACTIVITY MEASURES

An activity measure is an input, an output, or a physical attribute of an activity. For example, the input to the purchasing activity is a purchase requisition, and the output is a purchase order. The cost of the purchasing activity can be expressed as a cost per purchase requisition or purchase order. Other activity measures include:

Activity	Activity Measures
Accounts payable	Invoices
	Checks
Accounts receivable	Customer orders
	Number of customers
Inventory control	Number of part numbers
Material planning and control	Number of part numbers
Purchasing	Number of purchase orders
Receiving and component stores	Number of purchase orders
Incoming inspection	Number of inspections
Quality control	Number of inspections
Vendor evaluations	Number of vendors
Vendor certification	Number of vendors

Activity Measure
Characteristics

1. The ideal activity measure is simple to understand, easy to measure, easy to extract from existing data sources, and directly related to the activity's factors of production. It is critical that an activity measure be economically and practically available.

2. There must be a direct relationship between changes in the volume of an activity measure and the factors of production. The fixed/variable distinction has important implications that influence activity measures. It helps answer the following questions: Does a breakdown of activity measures occur with the approach of a step, and can the breakdown be predicted? Indeed, do these fundamental changes alter the definition of an activity? As activity volume varies with changes in organization, operations, technology, and sales, the factors of production will change accordingly. The changes in resources may occur in a stepwise manner depending on the factor's short-term or long-term influenceability and its capacity. When changes fundamentally affect how activities are performed, the activity measure must be reevaluated for its relevance.

3. Activity measures extend beyond direct production measures. For some activities, the number of direct labor hours will continue to be an appropriate activity measure. But there are many activity measures other than labor hours/cost within a department. For instance, machine hours may be relevant for highly automated departments, number of orders received or processed for the receiving department, number of physical measures (such as pounds, gallons, square meters) of orders shipped for the shipping department, number of set-ups and pounds of material moved for an indirect labor department.

4. By determining the output and users of activity information, the manager can determine whether specific activities are in service of short-range and/or long-term priorities. An accurate definition of current activities and desired outcomes is fundamental to acheiving those outcomes.

5. Knowing the cost per activity assists in planning and budgeting. Each organizational unit is analyzed to determine the current activities and cost per activity. This information represents the current level of service. The impact on the budget of changes in service level is easily identified.

Activity Measure or Cost Drivers

Whereas the activity measure represents the factor by which the costs of a given process vary most directly, the activity measure is not the cost driver. The cost driver is the factor whose occurrence creates cost. An activity measure is a dependent variable in the sense of a regression analysis.

To illustrate the difference, consider the activity of inserting components into electronics boards. As the number of inserts increases/decreases the factors of production (labor, technology, and the like) must be simultaneously adjusted. The activity measure is, therefore, the number of inserts. However, the number of inserts is caused by factors such as the product design and the available technology. These factors represent the cost drivers. The cost drivers are therefore the upstream causes of cost and are removed from the analyzed activity.

In the previous example, the number of inserts is a physical attribute of the insertion activity and thus meets the definition of an activity measure. It is a good activity measure because a *direct* correlation can be drawn between the number of inserts and the resources required to support the activity. On the other hand, an activity measure such as the number of components is related to a cost driver such as the product design. The measure is not directly correlated to the insertion activity and hence not a good activity measure. The number of components is an excellent factor to manage the need for insertions, but it is a *very inaccurate* mathematical basis for tracing cost.

SUMMARY

An activity cost is determined by examining each organizational unit to identify its business objectives, the individual work processes (activities), and the resources allocated to achieve its objectives. Activity costing therefore identifies the way a company uses its resources to accomplish its business objectives.

The traditional distinctions between fixed and variable and direct and indirect are secondary to the distinction between traceable and nontraceable costs.

8

CALCULATING AN ACTIVITY COST

The purpose of this chapter is to:

- Describe a six-step approach to calculating a product cost
- Describe and contrast the use of different cost types
- Describe typical cost categories and their relation to **natural expense categories**
- Explain how to determine an activity measure

An activity cost is calculated by tracing the total expense of all factors of production assigned to perform an activity. It is derived by defining an enterprise's activities and tracing the factors of production apportioned to each activity, and it is expressed in terms of an activity measure by which the cost of a given process varies most directly. Examples of activity measures include machine hours, number of inserts, and number of payroll checks. Finally, activity costs are traced to cost objectives such as products, processes, and orders based on the usage of the activity.

Graphically, the key steps in this process are shown on the following page.

STEP 1: SELECT COST BASIS

Selecting a cost basis involves the following steps:

- Determine cost type
- Determine cost time-horizon
- Classify life-cycle activities

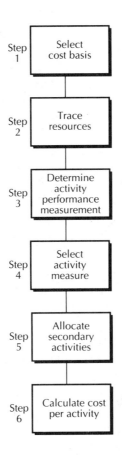

1a: Determine Cost Type

The first step in determining an activity cost is to determine the type of cost. An activity accounting system can use a variety of cost types such as actual, standard, budgeted, planned, or engineered. The choice of cost types is influenced by the type of cost in the existing accounting system, but this should not be the *only* factor influencing the choice.

The typical cost bases include the following:

Actual cost: An **actual cost** is the exact cost paid for a factor of production based on a financial transaction. The advantage of using an actual cost is that costs are always current and reflect changes in the business environment. The disadvantage is that actual costs are very sensitive to short-term fluctuations in the operating environment. Activity accounting will exacerbate this situation. In activity accounting an activity cost varies based on changes to both the cost of the factors of production and the volume of the activity measure. Cost reported under today's cost element–based cost systems varies primarily with changes in the cost of the factors of production because activity measures are not incorporated.

Budgeted cost: A **budgeted cost** reflects management's opinion, generally a most likely or hoped-for scenario, regarding future financial circumstances. A budget is the outcome of a periodic, structured planning process. It is used as a yardstick against which actual performance is measured. A budget encourages adherence to a plan and motivates different units in a firm toward the same goal. However, budgeted costs should be used with discretion as a basis for an activity accounting system because they represent what management *wants* to happen rather than what *does* happen.

Standard cost: A **standard cost** is a predetermined cost based on normal conditions of efficiency and volume of production. The cost is predetermined by either an analytical study or a management fiat. The advantage of a standard cost is that management control is directed only to costs that vary significantly between actual and standard (variance analysis).

Standard cost and its associated variance analysis often incite inappropriate behavior. For example, to achieve a favorable material price variance a purchasing officer would buy in large quantities. However, the storage and obsolescence costs associated with the stored material often exceed the cost savings attributable to the favorable price variance, and this results in less company profit. A source of this problem is that variance analysis assumes, often incorrectly, that cost control should be focused on the point of cost occurrence. In the purchase price variance example, the differences in purchase price at different quantity levels are the only cost-related considerations directly visible to the purchasing department. The cost of material movement, storage, and others are buried in other departments' budgets.

Standard cost systems control cost at an elemental level, resulting in an intermingling of different cost behavior patterns. The total cost of a factor of production such as labor, technology, or travel aggregates the total demand for the factor regardless of the number of activities supported. Also, standards do not portray life-cycle or business process–related decisions. Finally, standards are set relative to current operating conditions—not competition or the philosophy of continual improvement—thus incorporating current operating inefficiencies and non–value added activities into the standards.

Planned cost: A **planned cost** is derived from the strategic and operational planning systems. The output from the planning systems is a set of planning assumptions, including such factors as product sales forecasts, number of purchase orders to be processed, and others. The planning assumptions provide a superior basis for computing activity cost because the resulting planned cost provides the feedback necessary to ensure that planning assumptions are achieved or corrective action is initiated. What differentiates a planned cost from budgeted or standard costs is that it is continually derived from the operational systems. Budgeted and standard costs are typically derived on a yearly or semiannual basis.

Engineered cost: An **engineered cost** is derived from an industrial engineering study that provides insight into how an activity is performed and whether method improvements can increase performance. The advantage of such engineered data is that they are more reliable than subjective estimates. The disadvantage is that they are initially costly to develop: The procedure for developing engineering data is an event rather than a repetitive process, and it is difficult to reconcile with financial systems.

Most activity accounting systems use a predetermined cost such as standard, budgeted, or planned. Actual cost is not recommended because it is too sensitive to short-term fluctuations in activity volume. Engineered cost is an excellent source for estimating the initial activity cost of a new technology for which historical data are not available. Engineered cost is also outstanding for validating, on an ongoing basis, the reasonableness of activity cost when there is evidence that it might no longer mirror the manufacturing process.

Once a cost basis for an activity accounting system has been chosen, several changes must occur in the way most companies treat costs today. Primary among the changes are the following:

1. Costs must be set at the activity level.
2. Costs must separate the non–value added component of cost.
3. Costs must be summarized at the business process level to identify overall, companywide costs and to isolate cost drivers.

Whatever the cost basis used for an activity accounting system, it must be reconcilable with historical cost because it is essential that there be a consistent basis for comparing actual performance with planned performance.

However, the use of historical data in an activity accounting system is subtly but critically different from its use in a traditional management system. By custom, historical cost data have been used to project the future by extrapolating from past cost. In activity accounting, the cost behavior pattern of activities as they exist today are understood by tracing the factors of production to the activities that use the resources. Projecting a future cost is primarily a function of estimating the usage of the activity (as reflected in the activity measure) and changes to the cost of the factors of production. Unless the method of performing the activity is changed, the cost behavior pattern will remain constant.

1b: Determine Cost Time-Horizon

After the cost basis has been chosen, the next step is the selection of a time period for the cost data. Stability of data is an important consideration. Monthly data are very sensitive to short-term fluctuations. Anything less than yearly data is subject to seasonal fluctuations. For example, if one were to analyze the activities of a finance department in December, one might incorrectly assume that the department spends most of its time budgeting and closing the accounting records. Although yearly data is stable, it does not incorporate the dynamic changes to the business environment.

It is advisable to use quarterly or yearly data but continually adjust them for changes in the operating environment—reorganizations, modifications to activities, and the like. The monitoring of monthly variances between actual cost and planned cost at an aggregate department/cost center level—not at the activity level except in certain cases—facilitates a continual review of the dynamic business environment. Capturing actual cost at the activity level is both expensive and cumbersome. Monthly variances that are consistently skewed would indicate that planned costs are incorrect and should be reviewed.

In certain cases more precise data are required, and a company may choose to capture actual activity usage. Maintenance and repair activities might, for example, be traced to the specific equipment being serviced based on actual usage. Similarly, product design and manufacturing engineering are often directly tracked.

1c: Classify Life-Cycle Activities

Appropriate classification of activities and their costs into life-cycle segments is critical to activity accounting. Traditional accounting systems expense many costs associated with start-up, field operations, maintenance, product support, retirement, and disposal that should be capitalized and matched to the products they benefit. The rationale is that because the future is uncertain, predictions of future benefits are imprecise and a cost based conservatively on known events is superior to one based on forecasts.

Costs have historically been reported in small segments of time that provide a periodic "score card" of financial results—typically on a yearly basis. Periodic cost reporting results in a fragmented view of costs for products and processes whose value exceeds the reporting horizon. Product profitability, for example, is rarely computed over more than a year.

The conventional practice distorts product cost and leads to disjointed cost control. Life-cycle accounting provides a framework for the development and reporting of cost and performance over the useful life of significant assets. The life cycle commences with the initial identification of consumer needs and extends through planning, research, design, development, production, evaluation, use, logistics support in operation, retirement, and disposal. The cost of these life-cycle activities, in total, represents the product life-cycle cost. Assets for which life-cycle costs are normally computed include products, processes, projects, and systems.

Examples of life-cycle costs include the following:

Year of Asset's Life	Rearrangement of Facilities $	Industrial Engineering $	NC Programming $	Product Engineering $	Total Non-recurring $
1	40,000	25,000	15,000	40,000	120,000
2			20,000	50,000	70,000
3			25,000	40,000	65,000
4			10,000	20,000	30,000
5			5,000		5,000
Totals	$40,000	$25,000	$75,000	$150,000	$290,000

Life-cycle classification relates activities to the period when the benefits accrue and depicts the interdependencies of activities in different periods. For example, the output of the product design activity benefits the product over its entire life cycle. It also has a major impact on subsequent activities since, to a large extent, it limits the type of material and manufacturing processes that can be used. Therefore, the product design activity represents a life-cycle cost and should be apportioned to all units of a product sold over its life.

Life-cycle activities are classified as follows:

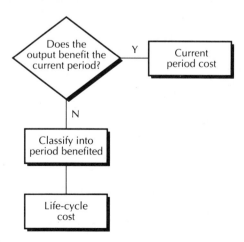

The benefits of production-related activities are realized in the current period and traced to the corresponding products. The benefits of support activities may benefit either the current or future period. A manufacturing engineering department, for example, may develop a product routing for a special, one-time customer order. The cost of the associated activities are traced directly to the specific customer order and are not capitalized. Other activities, such as process improvements, benefit future periods. For example, when a manufacturing engineering department develops a process plan for a new product to be marketed over several years, the cost of these activities should be charged over the entire product life cycle.

Still other activities may involve the development of a new flexible manufacturing cell. These costs are traceable to the manufacturing process life cycle and charged to products that use the new cell during its life.

Life-cycle accounting requires that initial cost estimates be time phased and expressed in constant monetary units (sterling, dollars, yen and so on) of the same base year. The constant monetary units should be adjusted periodically to reflect current (inflated) cost.

Activities provide an excellent foundation for a life-cycle management system because it is easy to determine whether an activity benefits current or future periods. Activities that benefit the current period are treated as an expense in the current period, and activities that benefit future periods should be capitalized.

STEP 2: TRACE RESOURCES

Cost is traced to activities by causal relationship. The key steps in tracing resources to activities include the following:

- Determine source of data.
- Group related general ledger costs.
- Establish causal relationship.
- Trace people-related costs.
- Trace all other costs to activities.

2a: Determine Source of Data

The primary source of cost data is a general ledger. Alternatively, cost data can be derived from a detailed industrial engineering analysis or estimated relationships between similar activities and the physical and performance characteristics of a system (parametric approach).

The structure of an activity accounting system permits costs to be derived by any of the three methods. In most cases the general ledger is the recommended source of cost information because the costs reported under the activity accounting system would reconcile to the financial reporting system. This is important since it ensures consistency between financial accounting data and the management system. Typically, engineering studies and parametric cost estimates are used to supplement the general ledger information, particularly when historical information is not available or is not representative of normal operations.

The cost source selected for the activity accounting system depends on the significance of the cost and availability of information. Where high cost or significant uncertainty exists, cost estimates may be derived by more than one of these techniques. Using multiple methods allows cross-checking and validation in which differently derived estimates are compared, analyzed, and judged.

The level of detail in the existing general ledger system rarely limits the cost analysis but rather impacts the level of effort required to translate department cost into activity costs. For example, the accounts payable function may be performed by a separate department in a large organization. Translating this cost into an accounts payable activity is straightforward. On the other hand, if accounts payable are the responsibility of a larger finance department, a higher level of effort would be required to extract these costs in an activity analysis. Each general ledger account would have to be analyzed to determine which finance department activity it supports. This would require significant effort, but eventually the accounts payable activity costs would be isolated.

2b: Group Related General Ledger Costs

A general ledger classifies expenses according to the types of expenditures. The tracing process is simplified by classifying cost in a department's general ledger with similar cost behavior patterns separated into **cost pools**. The entire cost pool can be input into the cost management system rather than requiring each cost element to be entered individually.

For example, consider technology costs. The cost of equipment capitalized on the balance sheet is normally limited to all the expenditures relating to its acquisition and preparation. This practice ignores factors such as the interest expense to finance the acquisition; nonrecurring costs such as software development, industrial engineering and product design; legal, numerical control programs, accounting, and consultant fees; and the cost of process R&D, which are associated with the manufacturing process. These costs are buried in numerous overhead accounts. When one considers the recurring costs of utilities, supplies, maintenance, and other support services, the total cost of technology is often 10 times as large as the initial investment. To hide these costs in numerous general ledger accounts is to mask their importance.

Because the decision to manufacture a product involves a long-term commitment to dedicate resources, it is important that the product cost system assign costs that reflect the actual amount of resources required to build a unit. For an accounting system to provide meaningful information it must mirror the manufacturing environment. In traditional product costing a key to accuracy is the breakdown of the manufacturing process and support departments into discrete cost pools to determine an appropriate basis for allocation.

Expenditures such as salary and wages, office supplies, depreciation, insurance, and similar items are accumulated by department or cost center. The number of accounts depends on the extent and detail of the information desired by management.

When the general ledger is chosen as the source of cost data, it is recommended that general ledger amounts with similar cost behavior patterns be summarized by natural expense category. For example, labor cost comprises salary, tax, withholding, and benefits accounts.

Natural expense categories include:

- Material
- Labor
- Technology
- Utilities
- Plant and facilities
- Information Systems
- Freight
- Travel
- Taxes
- Insurance
- Inventory

In this section we will discuss material, labor, and technology, and then turn to the category of intercompany activities.

Material

The cost of purchased material consists of the material purchase price and the expense of all other activities necessary to bring the material to the production process. This includes the cost of all activities related to the establishment, planning, acquisition, receiving, and control of raw materials and purchased components. Typical material-related expense categories include the following:

- *Material purchase price:* Planned purchase costs are developed by the purchasing department for each raw material and purchased component part number. These costs might include expected price increases depending on company policy.
- *Material price variance:* Difference between the actual and planned/standard purchase price.
- *Scrap:* When certain materials, rather than the manufacturing process, create scrap, these costs should be traced to the material.
- *Off-fall:* When the material content of the finished product is less than that of the raw materials, these off-fall costs should be traced to the material. Material off-fall results from the waste involved in cutting parts out of standard stock size and material removal operations such as grinding and milling.

Typical material-related activities include the following:

- *Purchasing:* The cost associated with the paperwork of placing a purchase order and the following up on its progress.
- *Receiving:* The cost of receiving and storing raw materials.
- *Incoming inspection:* The cost of inspecting incoming raw materials, including labor, cost of inspection equipment, facilities, and other traceable costs. If there is a standard sample, such as one piece per lot tested to destruction, the cost of the inspected material is associated with the material for each order.
- *Material movement:* All material movement costs, including freight and in-process material handling. A standard companywide freight cost percentage is used when freight cost does not vary significantly by individual order. When significant freight cost variations exist, however, they should be traced directly to the material ordered.
- *Material procurement support:* Includes vendor evaluation, vender certification, vender coordination, and material review board. The

costs associated with these activities are assigned to material cost as
vendor-related activities. It is often difficult to trace vendor-related
activities directly to specific material. These cost are normally treated
as secondary activities to the purchasing department and allocated to
the primary activities.

- *Accounts payable:* The accounts payable activity is part of the procurement process and should be traced to purchased material. It is
  recommended that the accounts payable activity be charged to products, using the number of purchase orders or purchase order lines as
  the activity measure.

Other material-related activities include the following:

- Quality control
- Component stores
- Inventory control
- Material planning and control
- Supervision
- Corporate materials management
- Manufacturing administration

Labor

Labor cost is the cost of all activities related to the acquisition, training,
and support of people. These would include fringe benefits, personnel,
training, cafeteria, and similar activities. Labor—both direct and support—
is traceable to activities. Labor costs are assigned to the activities using
information from the general ledger, payroll records, and staffing tables.
Typical labor-related expense categories include:

- *Salaries:* Salaries are the most significant component of an activity
  labor rate. Salary costs are traced at actual or standard rate by job
  classification.
- *Fringe benefits:* Fringe benefits for salaried and hourly employees are
  normally computed separately because of significant cost behavior pattern differences between the two groups.

Typical labor-related activities include:

- *Payroll:* It is recommended that the costs of this activity be traced to
  each department or work center according to headcount.

- *Human resources:* Human resources costs typically include recruiting and benefits administration. It is recommended that they be charged to each department and work center according to headcount.

Technology (process)

Technology cost is the cost of all activities necessary to acquire and operate the technology, including the cost of capital employed to finance the acquisition, start-up activities, operating activities, and directly impacted support activities. Technology costs include hardware, software, and related information system support activities and factors of production. Examples of technology costs include labor, depreciation, and energy. Technology-related support activities include NC programming and maintenance. Technology costs include both recurring and nonrecurring costs. The technology rate includes all traceable cost and uses an appropriate output measure that reflects actual usage, such as machine hours.

It is recommended that a technology bill of activities be prepared. The bill of activities defines all traceable technology-related activities and identifies the amount of each activity consumed by the technology. The amount of activity usage is based on the estimated volume of output for each activity. Technology costs represent the total operating cost at normal production volumes.

Typical technology-related expense categories include the following:

- *Acquisition cost:* The historical cost of the equipment based on fixed asset records and rental agreements.
- *Taxes:* Equipment-related taxes.
- *Interest expense:* The cost of financing the nonrecurring activities. The cost of capital is incurred regardless of whether the money is borrowed from an external source or from the shareholders.
- *Utilities/energy:* Direct charge (resource units per run hour; that is, kilowatt hour), used if significant; otherwise cost is included as part of occupancy cost.
- *Facilities:* Directly traced to processes (technologies) based on square footage. Detailed square footage is derived from engineering data. Total facilities-related costs and total plant square footage are used to calculate a cost per square foot.
- *Small tools:* Estimated yearly consumption used, or direct charge recorded in accounts payable as the small tools are acquired.
- *Supplies:* Estimated yearly consumption used or direct charge recorded in accounts payable as supplies are acquired.

Typical technology-related activities include the following:

- *Facilities cost:* The cost of the facilities required to house the technology.
- *Industrial engineering:* The cost of industrial engineering support to design the manufacturing process for the new technology.
- *NC programming:* The cost of initial programming and maintenance of programs used to control the numerically controlled equipment.
- *Process engineering:* The cost of engineers who program, debug, and repair equipment. This cost is directly charged to the technologies using these services based on estimated engineering hours or a project-costing system.
- *Machine operation:* The cost of the operator who tends the machine.
- *Supervision:* When significant time is dedicated to specific processes (technologies), supervision time is directly assigned. Otherwise, supervision time is allocated to all activities within the department. The percentage of labor cost by activity is a typical method of allocation.
- *Maintenance:* It is advisable to use estimated maintenance costs for preventive maintenance and to directly charge unplanned maintenance costs. Maintenance costs can be extracted from the preventive maintenance records and accounts payable for spare parts/outside service.
- *Leasing:* The cost of leased equipment should be traced to a manufacturing activity in the same manner as purchased equipment. Leased equipment differs from purchased equipment primarily in that its interest cost is reflected in the lease cost and not directly assigned to the activity.

Intercompany Activities

Some important intercompany activities include the following:

- *Use of management information system (MIS):* Total computer room operating costs, including hardware and software costs. Common methods of tracing MIS to the user departments include the number of reports or the amount of CPU time used. The costs of programming and system development are charged to activities based on actual usage of these resources.
- *Administrative support:* Administrative support costs are directly traced to the activity requesting the service.

Other intercompany activities include:

- Word Processing
- Facilities
- Industrial engineering
- NC programming
- Product engineering
- Maintenance

2c: Establish Causal Relationship

A causal relationship exists when a factor of production can be shown to be directly consumed by an activity. The key to establishing a causal relationship is defining an activity measure that is common to both the factor of production and the activity. Because people are paid on the basis of time, it is an excellent basis for costing people. Similarly, the amount of human resources consumed in an activity is normally stated in terms of time. Thus time is common to the factor of production and the activity.

Typical causal bases include:

Factor of Production	Measure
People	Time
Technology	Machine/technology hours
Facilities	Square footage
Utilities	Kilowatt hours

Reproducibility and completeness are important in establishing a causal relationship. *Reproducibility* refers to the analyst's responsibility to record what was done so that others may understand the ground rules and assumptions made, the analysis performed, and the results obtained. In this manner each estimate becomes both a self-contained, documented record of a complete cost estimate and a building block for future cost estimates.

Nontraceable costs are normally allocated to the primary activities to ensure completeness. *Completeness* refers to the communication of results in a format that encompasses the entire system, without the need for footnotes describing costs that were left out.

2d: Trace People-Related Costs

To trace people-related costs to activities requires information on:

1. The activities performed by the employee
2. The people-related cost for the department
3. A causal tracing basis

Techniques for defining activities were described in the activity analysis chapter (Chapter 6). The source of labor costs is either the general ledger or special engineering studies, as described earlier in this chapter. This section explains how labor is traced to specific activities.

Employee costs are traced to activities on the basis of either time or the physical output of the activity. The use of physical outputs as a basis for tracing employee cost is valid only if the effort to complete each individual output is homogenous. When employees work on several activities or outputs requiring differing amounts of effort, the time expended by employees on activities is the preferred basis.

The primary method of determining how a department spends its time is to interview the salaried supervisors responsible for managing an organizational unit. The number of employees supervised, the division of labor within the organizational unit, and activities performed are the key data to be extracted. In an activity accounting system it is unimportant whether the employee directly worked on the product or indirectly supported production—what is important is to trace workers' time to their activities.

The organization chart and its corresponding job descriptions provide an excellent starting point for tracing employee costs to activities. Through interviews, diaries/logs, engineering studies, or other appropriate techniques, each job classification is studied to determine which of the unit's activities the employee supports. The work activities of each group, or individual employee, are defined as illustrated in the figure on the following page.

Employee cost is traced to activities by multiplying the people-related cost by the time percentages determined during the activity analysis process. There are three primary methods for charging labor to activities:

1. Tracing total department employee cost to activities by using the percentage of time spent on each activity departmentwide.
2. Tracing employee cost to activities by using the percentage of time spent on each activity by a specific class of employee.
3. Tracing employee labor cost by using the percentage of time spent on each activity by each individual employee.

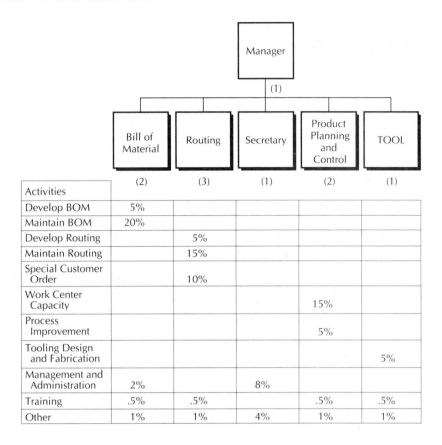

Activities	Bill of Material (2)	Routing (3)	Secretary (1)	Product Planning and Control (2)	TOOL (1)
Develop BOM	5%				
Maintain BOM	20%				
Develop Routing		5%			
Maintain Routing		15%			
Special Customer Order		10%			
Work Center Capacity				15%	
Process Improvement				5%	
Tooling Design and Fabrication					5%
Management and Administration	2%		8%		
Training	.5%	.5%		.5%	.5%
Other	1%	1%	4%	1%	1%

The choice of method depends on the degree of accuracy required. In a department where wages are relatively standard, the first approach is preferable because it is the simplest. When wages vary significantly within a department, the second and third methods are preferable.

To illustrate the difference in methods, assume an engineering department has the following staffing:

Job Type	Number of Employees	Total Salary $	Available Hours
Manager	1	60,000	2,000
Secretary	1	15,000	2,000
Design engineer	5	200,000	10,000
Engineer trainee	3	60,000	6,000
Total	10	$335,000	20,000

For the sake of this example, assume the activity analysis identified the following activities of the engineering department:

- New product design
- Engineering change notices (ECNs)
- Training
- Management and administration
- Other

Total Labor Method

Under the total labor method, employee-related cost is distributed to activities by multiplying the total department salaries and employee-related cost by the percentage of time spent on each activity. The total department salary is $335,000. Assume the activity analysis determined the following departmentwide breakdown of time:

Activity	Time %
New product design	25
ECN	35
Training	10
Management and administration	15
Other	15
Total	100%

The $335,000 department labor cost is distributed to the activities according to the total department activity time percentages. Alternatively, the employee hours spent on each activity could be used, which would result in the same **cost assignment**. The distribution results in the following assignment of labor costs to activities:

Activity	Cost $	
New product design	83,750	(335,000 × 0.25)
ECN	117,250	(335,000 × 0.35)
Training	33,500	(335,000 × 0.10)
Management and administration	50,250	(335,000 × 0.15)
Other	50,250	(335,000 × 0.15)
Total	$335,000	

Occupational Code Method

Under the occupational code method, salary and employee-related cost are distributed to the department's activities by multiplying the total employee-related cost in each occupational code by the corresponding percentage of time spent on the activity.

The first step in the occupational code method is to determine the labor grades within a department. The labor grades provide insight into the types of activities the workers perform. The departmental managers or an engineering study identifies, for each occupational code, the key activities and percentage of total time spent on each activity. A rate per hour for each occupational code is computed by dividing the average salary by the number of productive hours available. For example, consider the engineering department:

Job Type	Number of Employees	Occupational Code	Average Salary $	Hourly Rate $
Manager	1	001	60,000	30.00
Secretary	1	002	15,000	7.50
Design engineer	5	003	40,000	20.00
Engineer trainee	3	004	20,000	10.00

An analysis of time spent by each class of employee in the engineering department results in the following breakdown of time:

Activity	Occupational Code	Hours
New product design	003	5,000
ECN	003	3,000
	004	4,000
Training	003	800
	004	1,200
Management and administration	001	1,400
	002	1,600
Other	001	600
	002	400
	003	1,200
	004	800
Total		20,000

The next step is to multiply the hours for each activity/occupational code by the occupational code rate as follows:

Activity	Occupational Code	Hours	Cost $	
New product design	003	5,000	100,000	(5,000 × 20.00)
ECN	003	3,000	60,000	(3,000 × 20.00)
	004	4,000	40,000	(4,000 × 10.00)
Training	003	800	16,000	(800 × 20.00)
	004	1,200	12,000	(1,200 × 10.00)
Management and administration	001	1,400	42,000	(1,400 × 30.00)
	002	1,600	12,000	(1,600 × 7.50)
Other	001	600	18,000	(600 × 30.00)
	002	400	3,000	(400 × 7.50)
	003	1,200	24,000	(1,200 × 20.00)
	004	800	8,000	(800 × 10.00)
Total		20,000	$335,000	

The distribution results in the following assignment of labor costs to activities:

Activity	Cost $
New product design	100,000
ECN	100,000
Training	28,000
Management and administration	54,000
Other	53,000
Total	$335,000

Specific Employee Method

Under the specific employee method, all supervisors and employees are interviewed or an engineering study is conducted to understand their activities and responsibilities and to determine the time spent on key activities. Assume the analysis revealed the following breakdown:

Employee	Salary $	Activity				
		NPD %	ECN %	TRN %	M&A %	OTH %
Manager	60,000				0.70	0.30
Secretary	15,000				0.80	0.20
Senior design engineer	60,000	0.80				0.20
Design engineer 1	40,000	0.65	0.25			0.10
Design engineer 2	40,000	0.65	0.25			0.10
Junior design engineer 1	30,000	0.20	0.50	0.20		0.10
Junior design engineer 2	30,000	0.20	0.50	0.20		0.10
Senior engineer trainee 1	22,500		0.80			0.20
Senior engineer trainee 2	22,500		0.80			0.20
Junior engineer trainee	15,000		0.40	0.60		

Where NPD = New product design
       ECN = Engineering changes
       TRN = Training
       M&A = Management and administration
       OTH = Other

A total activity cost is determined by multiplying the activity percentages by the employee's salary and summing by activity.

Employee	Activity				
	NPD $	ECN $	TRN $	M&A $	OTH $
Manager				42,000	18,000
Secretary				12,000	3,000
Senior design engineer	48,000				12,000
Design engineer 1	16,000	10,000			4,000
Design engineer 2	26,000	10,000			4,000
Junior design engineer 1	6,000	15,000	6,000		3,000
Junior design engineer 2	6,000	15,000	6,000		3,000
Senior engineer trainee 1		18,000			4,500
Senior engineer trainee 2		18,000			4,500
Junior engineer trainee		6,000	9,000		
Total	$112,000	$92,000	$21,000	$54,000	$56,000

Comparing the three methods yields the following results on the next page.

Using the total labor approach, we can conclude that activities requiring more senior people are undercosted because an average wage rate is used.

Activity	Total Labor $	Occupation Code $	Specific Employee $
New product design	83,750	100,000	112,000
ECN	117,250	100,000	92,000
Training	33,500	28,000	21,000
Management and administration	50,250	54,000	54,000
Other	50,250	53,000	56,000

Although the highest accuracy is obtained by tracing specific employees to activities, this approach is not recommended for widespread use because it is too cumbersome and expensive. To begin with, a time-reporting system would have to be installed. Second, specific employee data are subject to short-term fluctuations in skill levels applied to activities, and this distorts activity costs.

The cost per activity is based on the planned level of employee experience necessary to perform an activity. Use of more-experienced people should require less time (at a higher rate), whereas use of less-experienced people should require more time (at a lower rate). The net cost, time multiplied by rate, represents a variance from plan.

Cost information by employee occupation code normalizes the data. Thus, it is advisable to use occupation codes. It is important that the salary range of each occupation code be carefully constructed so as not to allow significant variations.

Trace All Other Costs to Activities

After employee-related cost is traced to activities, each cost category is investigated through interviews and a review of records to identify the activity that caused the cost to be incurred. In our example, costs are traced to activities as illustrated in the figure on the following page.

Not all costs are cost-effectively traced to activities. These *nontraceable* costs represent general department/cost center support costs. To directly charge 100 percent of a department's costs to activities is seldom possible or cost-effective. As a rule of thumb, a company should strive to directly trace between 80 to 90 percent of its costs to activities.

The remaining nontraceable costs are general departmental costs. Being related to a specific department, they should not be allocated on the basis of a company wide cost pool. Therefore, it is recommended that a department's nontraceable costs be allocated to the organization's primary activities on the basis of the department's primary factor of production.

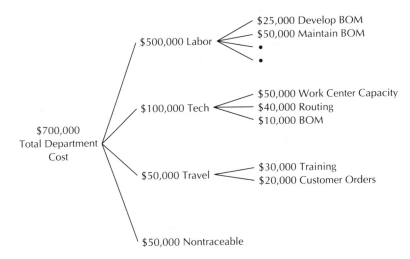

For example, the nontraceable costs for the engineering department ($50,000) would be allocated to activities using labor costs—the department's primary factor of production. The costs would be allocated as follows:

Activities	Time %	Allocated Costs $
Develop bill of material	5	2,500
Maintain bill of material	20	10,000
Develop routing	5	2,500
Maintain routing	15	7,500
Special customer order	10	5,000
Work center capacity	15	7,500
Process improvement	5	2,500
Tooling design and fabrication	5	2,500
Management and administration	10	5,000
Training	2	1,000
Other	8	4,000

STEP 3: DETERMINE ACTIVITY PERFORMANCE MEASUREMENT

Activities are described in terms of both financial and nonfinancial performance measures. Activity accounting considers cost and nonfinancial performance information as attributes of an activity. Performance measures address questions about an activity such as:

- What does it cost?
- How much time does it take (actual and elapsed)?
- How well is the activity performed?
- How flexible is the activity in response to changes in the manufacturing environment?

Each view provides a different insight into the activity. A commonly used analogy is to several windows through which to view activities. One window (view) shows an activity in terms of the cost of performing it. Another window (view) shows an activity in terms of the time required to perform it. Other common views include flexibility, quality, and schedule attainment.

The relationship among performance measures is tightly bonded, so that a change to an activity simultaneously impacts all aspects of performance measures. A reduction in time, for example, will impact cost, quality, and flexibility because it impacts the way in which the activity is performed. As a consequence of the interrelationships of performance measures, it is misleading to judge activity performance by a single measure in isolation from the others.

To optimize the performance of the enterprise as a whole requires considering the impact of relationships among performance measures. Consider cost. One method of reducing cost is to increase output using the same amount of resources. If this goal is accomplished at the expense of quality, the cost reduction achieved in one department is offset by additional activities to correct the problem in downstream departments. The total company performance is diminished.

A key to effective cost management is to implement changes that improve multiple dimensions of performance simultaneously. This is only possible when the activity accounting tightly couples nonfinancial and financial measures.

STEP 4: SELECT ACTIVITY MEASURE

Selecting an activity measure involves the following steps:

- Determine activity measure.
- Gather statistics on output/transactions.
- Validate activity measure for reasonableness.

4a: Determine Activity Measure

As discussed earlier, activity measures are inputs, outputs, or physical attributes of an activity. Surrogate activities are used when it is infeasible to use the best activity measure.

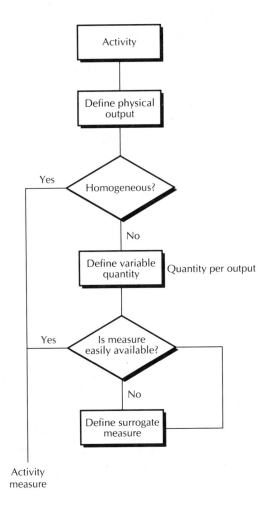

It is a common phenomenon that the greater the desired accuracy, the more difficult it is to obtain activity data to achieve it. Determining the total number of purchase orders, for example, is simpler than determining the number of purchase order line items. In many cases, the activity accounting system must trade off the advantages of greater accuracy against the increased data collection costs.

Several activities might be aggregated into a surrogate activity measure in which no activities are significant enough on their own to warrant separate management. Similarly, an activity measure might be chosen that is not the most accurate mathematical basis for tracing costs, because it is infeasible to collect volume statistics for the most appropriate measure. The disadvantage of using surrogate activities and activity measures is that they represent an imperfect compromise between the simplicity of the system and the resulting cost distortion.

It is important to choose a surrogate activity measure that will closely approximate the cost behavior of the activity or motivate a specified behavior. An example of a surrogate activity measure that will approximate a cost behavior is the use of purchase orders when the number of purchase order lines might be more appropriate. A behavior activity measure is used only when a surrogate measure cannot be found that closely approximates the cost behavior.

4b: Gather Statistics on Output/Transactions

After an activity measure has been selected, the frequency of its occurrence is determined. The following are two common sources of activity volume information:

- Data processing transaction statistics.
- Department records. If production orders are numbered sequentially, for example, an approximation of the number of production orders is determined by subtracting the beginning number from the ending number.

It is important that the period of time used for the activity volume statistics correspond to the same time period used in determining the cost basis.

Activity	Activity Measure	Volume
Accounts payable	Invoices	100,000
	Checks	65,000
Accounts receivable	Customer orders	20,000
	Number of customers	8,000

Activity Measure Considerations

The identification of an appropriate activity measure is critical to the successful implementation of an activity accounting system. Two key factors to be considered when selecting an activity measure include:

- Activity measure homogeneity
- Relative costs of the aggregate activity

Activity measure homogeneity: An activity measure is said to be homogeneous when each output is of the same kind as the others. This means that the output must have consistent cost behavior patterns and require similar amounts of the factors of production. One test for homogeneity is the variability of the cost per unit. For example, a purchase order is a good activity measure for the purchase order activity only if the cost of each individual purchase order does not vary dramatically from others. This condition is not valid if a company generates both complex and simple purchase orders depending on the product. Clearly the production of a complex purchase order is more resource-intensive than the production of a simple purchase order. In this case, a purchase order is not a homogeneous activity measure. Instead the number of purchase order lines is a more appropriate activity measure.

The homogeneity of an activity measure can be determined by calculating the cost per activity for a random sample of the occurrences of an activity. If the cost per measure does not vary over 20 percent, the activity measure can be considered homogeneous.

The importance of activity measure homogeneity can be seen by the impact it has on product cost. For example, assume a purchasing department is incurring $150,000 to process 10,000 purchase orders. It might be concluded that the cost per purchase order is $15. However, a purchase order varies in complexity from 1-line item to 200 line items. The amount of resources required for a 1-line item purchase order is much less than for the 200-line purchase order.

To continue the example, the average purchase order contains 20 line items. The cost per line item is, therefore, $0.75. This means that the cost for a 1-line item purchase order would be closer to $0.75 than $15. Similarly, the cost for a 200-line item purchase order would be closer to $150 than $15. Unless most purchase orders contain approximately 20 line items, the resulting product cost distortion is significant.

The greater the heterogeneity of activities, the greater the distortion that is introduced. Products that are high consumers of purchase order line items are undercosted, whereas products that are low consumers of line items are overcosted.

Relative cost of the activity: The relative cost of the activity is a very important factor in selecting an activity measure. If the impact of an activity on total cost is insignificant, the resulting product cost distortion is minimal and a surrogate activity measure is appropriate. The relative impact of an activity on total cost depends on how large the activity cost is as a percentage of the total cost of the product, process, or other reporting objective.

To illustrate this point, assume an activity accounts for 20 percent of the total cost of a particular product. An inappropriate activity measure that traces twice as much cost to the product than would a valid output measure would therefore cause reported product costs to be 20 percent too high. However, if the activity accounts for only 0.2 percent of total cost, then the distortion introduced is only 0.2 percent.

The purchase order example can be modified to demonstrate the effect of a relatively large cost impact of an activity on reported product costs for several products. Assume that the cost for the simple product was $120 and $1,500 for the complex product. The product costs were computed using the average $15 purchase order cost. The revised product cost using the cost per purchase order line is $106 (120 − 15 + 0.75) for the simple product and $1,635 (1,500 − 15 + 150) for the complex product. The simple product is overcosted by 12 percent whereas the complex product is undercosted by 9 percent. It can be concluded that the purchase order cost is a significant percentage of total cost and the selection of an appropriate activity measure is critical.

4c: Validate Activity Measure for Reasonableness

The activity measure must be validated to ensure that relationships between the activity cost and activity levels as represented by the activity measure are valid. Alternative activity measures should be selected in cases where lack of homogeneity is detected. It is important to separate out changes in the cost of resources due to technology changes, improved labor skills, or price level changes.

A number of techniques are available to validate activity measures for reasonableness. The primary ones include the following:

- *High-low approach,* which examines cost behavior at the highest and lowest levels of activity

- *Curve fitting,* which determines the line that best explains the relationship between changes in cost and the activity level by graphing historical relationships or using statistical regression analysis
- *Multiple regression analysis,* which is similar to curve fitting but is used when changes in costs are a function of multiple independent variables

Before a regression analysis of costs (the dependent variable) against volume (the independent variable) can properly be made, the costs should be adjusted to consider (among other possible considerations) inflation, seasonality, strikes, vacation shutdowns, annual salary and wage increases, and accounting period anomalies. These adjustments are complex (consider seasonality, for instance), and most financial accounting systems do not easily adapt to such corrections. In fact, some expenses are often prorated over accounting periods (such as months or quarters) with the specific purpose of eliminating observable seasonal variations.

A simple regression rarely produces a completely desirable coefficient of regression because of the influence of cost drivers other than the single independent variable assumed in linear regression. Although a multiple correlation may eventually identify a relationship between the studied cost and some number of independent variables, the complexities introduced by such a calculation make the process impractical for regular use by management.

STEP 5: ALLOCATE SECONDARY ACTIVITIES

Primary activities contribute directly to the mission of the organizational unit and are used outside the enterprise or by another organizational unit within the company. Secondary activities support the primary activities. They include management, training, general meetings, and administration.

Because secondary activities support the primary activities, they are allocated to the primary activities rather than to general company overhead. A common method is to allocate secondary activities to the primary activities using the primary factors of production (see the table on the following page).

STEP 6: CALCULATE COST PER ACTIVITY

Once a company has traced cost to an activity, selected an output measure, and determined the quantity of the activity measure, it can complete the activity costing process. To illustrate this, consider a procurement department

Activities	P/S	Time %	Allocated Costs $	
Bill of material (development)	P	5	625	($\frac{5}{80}$ × 10,000)
Bill of material (maintenance)	P	20	2,500	($\frac{20}{80}$ × 10,000)
Routing (development)	P	5	625	($\frac{5}{80}$ × 10,000)
Routing (maintenance)	P	15	1,875	($\frac{15}{80}$ × 10,000)
Special customer order	P	10	1,250	($\frac{10}{80}$ × 10,000)
Work center capacity	P	15	1,875	($\frac{15}{80}$ × 10,000)
Process improvement	P	5	625	($\frac{5}{80}$ × 10,000)
Tooling design and fabrication	P	5	625	($\frac{5}{80}$ × 10,000)
Management and administration	S	10		
Training	S	2		
Other	S	8		

that spends $120,000 processing 6,000 purchase orders. The average cost per purchase order is $20. A complex product requires $400 (20 purchase orders at $20) of the purchase order activity, whereas the simple product requires $20 (1 purchase order at $20)—dramatic differences.

The final step is to sum the extended unit cost of each traceable activity and allocated portion of nontraceable costs.

1. Obtain total cost for the activity from the general ledger.
2. Obtain total volume of activity measures.
3. Divide step 1 results by step 2 results to obtain the cost per activity measure.

$$\text{Activity cost} = \frac{\text{Traceable resources} + \text{Secondary activity}}{\text{Activity measure quantity}}$$

In the accounting department example, the activity costs would be calculated as follows:

Activity	Activity Measure	Activity Cost	Volume	Cost per Activity
Accounts payable	Invoices	$133,000	100,000	$1.33/invoice
	Checks		65,000	$2.46/check
Accounts receivable	Customer orders	$ 80,000	20,000	$4.00/customer order
	Number of customers		8,000	$10.000/customer

It is important to note that an activity cost is a productivity measure— inputs divided by outputs. As such, all the activities of the entire enterprise are measured in terms of productivity measures.

ACTIVITY COST EXAMPLE

Step 1: Extract the accounting department cost from the general ledger.

Accounting Department	$
Labor	500,000
MIS	100,000
Travel	100,000
Others	100,000
Total	$800,000

Step 2: Determine the activities of the accounting department:

Accounts payable	Cost accounting
Accounts receivable	Management
General financial reports	Training
Payroll	Other

Step 3: Define percentage of time expended on each activity:

Accounting Department	%
Accounts payable	20
Accounts receivable	20
General financial reports	15
Payroll	15
Cost accounting	10
Management	5
Training	5
Other	10

Step 4: Trace cost to the specific activities using the total department method for the labor:

Accounting Department	Labor $	Travel $
Accounts payable	100,000	
Accounts receivable	100,000	
General financial reports	75,000	20,000
Payroll	75,000	
Cost accounting	50,000	
Management	25,000	
Training	25,000	30,000
Other	50,000	

Step 5: Allocate secondary costs to activities using labor time as the basis of allocating cost:

Accounting Department		$
Accounts payable	100,000 × 0.22	= 22,000
Accounts receivable	100,000 × 0.22	= 22,000
General financial reports	95,000 × 0.17	= 16,150
Payroll	75,000 × 0.17	= 12,750
Cost accounting	50,000 × 0.11	= 5,500
Management	25,000 × 0.055	= 1,375
Training	55,000 × 0.055	= 3,025
Other	50,000 × 0.11	= 5,500

Step 6: Determine total cost for the activity:

Accounting Department	Labor $	Travel $	Management $	Total $
Accounts payable	100,000		22,000	122,000
Accounts receivable	100,000		22,000	122,000
General financial reports	75,000	20,000	16,150	
Payroll	75,000		12,750	
Cost accounting	50,000		5,500	
Management	25,000		1,375	
Training	25,000	30,000	3,025	
Other	50,000		5,500	55,500

SUMMARY

Activities provide the building blocks for tracing costs to reporting objectives. Specifying all the activities necessary to accomplish a business function provides the basis for understanding cost. To build a product might, for example, require activities such as research and development, product design, facilities modification, and field support in addition to the activities associated with the physical production process. The sequence of activities is known as the bill of activities.

9

TRACING ACTIVITY COST

The purpose of this chapter is to:

- Describe the weakness of the conventional reporting methods
- Identify business decisions using an activity accounting system
- Identify reporting objectives
- Describe how to trace costs
- Describe how to construct a bill of activities
- Discuss the importance of cost precision and cost significance in the decision-making process

Cost is meaningful only when it is related to an enterprise mission. Knowing the cost of building a product, placing an order, managing a department, or satisfying external reporting requirements facilitates the decision-making process. The objective for which cost information is needed (product, order, department, external reporting requirements, and the like) is known as the final cost objective.

Costs are linked to a final cost objective by a causal relationship. To do something such as to build a product or process an order involves activities. For example, building a product involves design, definition of the manufacturing process, procurement of the material, transformation of raw material through various manufacturing processes, shipping, and maintenance at the customer location.

Activities provide the basis for costing. An activity is the most basic unit of cost and can be summarized in numerous formats to support various reporting requirements.

The process of identifying specific activities and determining how much of each activity is consumed in the final cost objective is known as **tracing**. Tracing cost to the end user has two primary objectives: to understand the current cost structure and to determine whether alternative activities might be superior.

The number of possible reporting objectives is immense. Different management decisions require different levels of cost detail and therefore different cost roll-ups. Consider the make/buy decision. Knowing the cost of building a product or component enables a company to compare that cost with the cost of purchasing it from an outside source.

A company must continually evaluate the cost-effectiveness of each activity to determine whether to restructure the activity or to purchase it externally. In the long run a company will liquidate and reallocate resources from an activity center that fails to satisfy customers efficiently, whether they be inside or outside the company. To do otherwise would diminish the company's long-term profitability.

In a cost management system, the role of cost accounting is to ensure that the information necessary to support the decision process is collected as completely and efficiently as possible and made available in the right form at precisely the right time. This requires that the cost management system be derived from and integrated with the company's decision support system.

TRADITIONAL REPORTING OBJECTIVES

Traditionally, a primary use of cost accounting information was for inventory valuation to support external financial reporting. Thus accounting methods are chosen on criteria such as consistency, simplicity, and conservatism. Accounting was used primarily as a "report card" to depict what happened after the costs were incurred. The new emphasis of cost management is to control cost by predicting cost behavior patterns during the planning stage and tracking actual results against the plan during the execution stage to initiate corrective action where required.

In the conventional cost accounting system, the process of attaching costs to cost objectives requires an extensive number of allocations. The reason is that costs are aggregated in large cost pools by cost element. To assign cost from aggregate cost pools to cost objectives necessitates numerous allocations that are often selected on criteria like regulatory requirements and ease of operations.

The accounting treatments of cost are often dissimilar for different decisions. Traditional cost accounting requires the development of a separate cost accounting system for each different view of cost. For example, an assest may use double-declining depreciation for tax purposes and straight line for financial reporting. The choice of depreciation methods will impact cost throughout the life of the asset, resulting in separate-period reporting. Separate accounting systems are thus required for tax and financial reporting purposes.

Dissimilar accounting methods promote the inherently non–value added cost of maintaining separate systems. The compromise that most companies choose is to operate a single system to support the multiple reporting objectives. Such a system requires the choice of one dominant accounting method on which to base cost.

For example, charging the cost of software development to the current period is conservative and would be most appropriate in reporting external financial results. Alternatively, capitalizing the development better matches cost to future products and better mirrors the manufacturing process—an important requirement for internal decision making. However, with a single system, the company must choose between external reporting requirements (conservative bias) and management control (better matching bias).

USES OF ACTIVITY ACCOUNTING

Activity accounting accommodates diverse reporting and cost control objectives. Having identified activities and their output, traced costs to activities, and computed a cost per activity, a company is positioned to identify the users of activities. Activity information can be summarized in numerous ways by tracing the activities to the reporting objectives. The viewpoints chosen depend on the scope and objectives of the cost control or reporting objective. Consider the decisions shown in the table on the following page.

Reporting Objectives

Typical reporting objectives include organizational units, orders, cost control units, products, projects, functions, and business processes. An explanation of each of these reporting objectives is included here:

Product: The cost of all activities involved in designing, manufacturing, and distributing a product.

Product Line: The cost of all activities unique to each family of products. A product line consists of a number of product models or product families. Marketing organizations normally forecast in terms of models, and management thinks in terms of models.

Order: The cost of all activities involved in acquiring and processing a customer or production order. Order costs represent a one-time cost per order and are relatively fixed irrespective of the order quantity. When the cost of an order is large relative to the cost per unit, the profitability of the order is highly dependent on the order size. For example, if the order cost is $100 per order and the customer is buying one $100 product, then the total cost to the company is $200 for the unit of product. However, if the

Decisions	Focus
Cost control	Predictive cost and performance
Make/buy	Predictive cost and performance Vendor price and performance Risk
Estimating	Predictive cost and performance
Pricing	Product cost Target cost
Investment analysis	Cost/benefit of new process Risk
Manufacturing planning and control	Resource allocation and constraints
Design to cost	Predictive cost and performance
Location analysis	Differences in factors of production cost
Product line analysis	Predictive cost and performance Product line cost
Marketing mix	Advertising, promotion, selling
Salesperson	Performance, evaluation, compensation plan
Channels of distribution	Type of activity
Abandonment analysis	Predictive cost and performance Product line cost
Customer	Volume or order size
Budgeting/forecasting	Corporate goals Predictive cost and performance with varying levels of support
Acquisitions/divestitures	Strong/weak activities Forecast of demand for activities

customer orders 50 of the same product, the cost to the company would be $102 per unit of product.

Decisions on order quantity are made by consumers and the marketing department. The conventional practice of including the order cost in overhead and allocating it to all products obscures a key determinant of profitability.

Two important activities that should be traced to orders are accounts receivable and credit and collections:

- *Accounts receivable:* The cost of processing accounts receivable is directly related to a customer order.
- *Credit and collections:* The cost of credit checking and collecting the outstanding receivables represents a cost directly attributable to specific customers or a customer order. However, when the activity

is directly related to tracking down problems related to poor product quality or mispriced orders, the cost of the activity should be included as part of the company cost of quality.

Administrative: The cost of all activities necessary to manage an enterprise including external compliance and reporting requirements. Administrative costs should be separated into department-related and corporate administration costs. These costs should be assigned to products based on the activities that cause the need for administration. For example, administration of quality activities would be assigned to quality activities based on where the administration effort is expended.

It is common practice to allocate corporate administration—including cost accounting, internal reporting, and financial analysis required for managing a company—to products. The resulting administrative allocation is often equated to a franchise fee.

Organizational unit: An enterprise functions through its organizational structure. Managers have significant influence over the efficiency and effectiveness of the activities in their area of responsibility. They control how activities are accomplished and select or influence the selection of the factors of production to perform the work. The degree of influenceability varies according to timing and company policy. Fixed factors of production such as machines, equipment, and information systems are normally changed only in the long run. However, they are traceable to the activity and are therefore *controllable*.

Cost control unit: The cost control unit represents the cost of *all* activities resulting from decisions made by an organization, even though the costs were incurred in other organizational units. It represents the cost driver. Managing cost requires understanding the underlying cause-and-effect relationship between the cause of cost and its occurrence.

Cost management systems that report costs only at the point of cost occurrence misdirect company resources by treating symptoms rather than solving problems. They also depend on the managers' ability to understand associated cost drivers. In other words, effective cost management requires a focus on the *source* of costs. Only by addressing the source can costs be minimized.

Marketing: Activity-based marketing analysis traces costs based on activities required to support the sales territory, salesperson, and size of orders. Conventional practices equate selling efficiency with increased sales volume as an indication of increased profitability. The idea is that more is better. However, too frequently increased sales volume does not equal increased profit.

Activity-based marketing cost analysis stresses profits rather than the traditional sales volume as a basis for decisions and evaluation of marketing. It aids in controlling costs by first associating the cost of all specific marketing activities to the benefiting cost objective (sales territory, customer, distribution channel and so on).

Traceable marketing costs are those incurred for and benefiting a single segment of sales and are easily associated with specific commodities or sales segments. Accordingly, the cost to operate a district sales office is a direct cost of the sales territory in which the office is located. Nontraceable costs are those incurred for and benefiting sales generally but not traceable to specific products or sales units.

Customer: The cost of supporting specific customers is determined by tracing all activities required to support the customer. Some customers are more expensive to serve than others. Consider the following:

Type of Customer	Characteristics
Distributor	Many units per order One shipping destination Few returns
Retail	Few units per order Many shipping destinations Many returns Consumer packaging Promotional programs

It is important to be able to answer the following questions:

- What does each channel of distribution really cost?
- Which channel provides the best service to the customers?
- What can be done to lower costs and improve service?
- Are certain specific customers more or less expensive?

The first step in a customer analysis is to classify customers into groups based on sales volume, product mix, and buying characteristics. Typical classifications include:

- Distributors
- National accounts
- Buying groups
- Independent dealers

When analyzing customer-specific activities and costs consider whether specific customers/channels require more or less support for the following activities or costs:

- Salespeople and sales commissions
- Warehouse
- Freight
- Accounts receivable (Do specific customers/channels take longer to pay their accounts and thus require more capital to finance?)
- Shipping office
- Shipping dock
- Finished goods inventory
- Distribution center shipping office
- Order entry
- Insurance
- Returns
- Discounts
- Advertising
- Trade shows
- Promotions
- Literature
- Billing
- Product liability and legal representation
- Credits

Business function: A business function is an aggregation of activities that are related by common purpose. Quality and security are examples of business functions.

Most companies are organized by the major functions of finance, engineering, marketing, management, and manufacturing. However, the total spectrum of activities for a business function is much broader than the organizational unit responsible for the function.

Business functional analysis aggregates related activities that would otherwise be hidden in numerous departments. This is accomplished by classifying each activity by the function of which it is a subset. For example, the activities of the quality department are part of the quality function, but there are many other quality-related activities, such as quality planning, in-process inspection, and customer feedback, that occur in other departments. Determining the total cost of quality would necessitate knowing the cost of all these activities regardless of the department in which they are performed. Knowing the total cost for significant functions focuses management's attention on identifying solutions that transcend organizational boundaries.

A functional cost analysis is also a valuable budgeting tool because it identifies requirements for activities that are not part of the department's normal activities. Consider the impact of a change in policies relating to in-process inspection. A production department would have to perform additional in-process inspection activities that would take away time from normal production activities. If the source of the requirements is unknown, the department's productivity would appear to have decreased.

A sample functional roll-up of quality-related activities into a cost of quality follows:

Incoming inspection
Vendor liaison/problem solving
Training (quality department)
Producibility analysis
Administration (quality department)
Source surveillance
In-process inspection
Production surveillance
Production troubleshooting
Production corrective action
Rework
Scrap/spoilage
Obsolescence
TQM program
Final inspection
Quality planning
Quality audit
Material analysis

Project: A project is a chain of activities interconnected by time to accomplish a specific objective such as the installation of a new manufacturing process or computer system. The cost of a project can be thought of as a collection of the activity costs necessary to complete the project.

WHICH REPORTING OBJECTIVES?

The cost objective depends on the decision to be made. A matrix of decisions and cost objectives portrays this relationship in the table on the following page.

TRACEABILITY CRITERIA

Traceable activities should be distinctly identified in the final reporting objective. Traceable activities have an established cause-and-effect relationship with a reporting objective. Therefore, the cost of all traceable activities that support the final cost objective is relevant to the final decision involving the cost objective.

Consider a painting activity. The primary cost for a human to paint a component would consist of the time expended multiplied by the laborer's rate. Conversely, the primary cost for a robot to paint a component would consist of the time expended multiplied by the robot's rate. In either case the component that was painted is unaffected by whether the painting was done by a human or a robot. An indisputable cause-and-effect relationship is established between the amount of paint and the product. The traceability criterion has been established. The secondary costs associated with painting include supplies, facilities, and support equipment.

In an activity accounting system it is important that all costs be traced where practical and economically feasible. A rule of thumb is that 80 to 90 percent of a department's costs should be traceable to the activities of the department. Tracing less than 80 to 90 percent does not provide the breakdown necessary to manage costs; tracing more is uneconomical. However, nontraceable costs should be clearly separated. The remaining 10 to 20 percent of cost is considered nontraceable. Nontraceable cost can be allocated if a fully absorbed cost is important to the final decision.

A critical factor in decision making is relevance. Traceability and relevance are synonymous. Decisions involve alternatives—relevance determines which costs and activities are considered and which are excluded. Traceable costs are controllable because a cause-and-effect relationship is established. Each alternative is evaluated in terms of its impact on traceable costs, because traceable activities will differ among each activity.

Traceability helps bring management pressures to bear on overhead or shared costs (for example SG&A, engineering, manufacturing, and corporate overhead) that are otherwise difficult to evaluate and control. When companies allocate these costs to specific products or cost centers, they

Decision	Activity Analysis	Cost Objective							
		Product	Order	Administration	Process	Organization	Market	Project
Make/buy	X	X	X					
Estimating	X	X					X	X
Investment analysis	X				X	X	X	X
Manufacturing planning and control	X		X		X			
Design to cost	X	X					X	X
Location analysis	X						X	X
Product line analysis	X	X	X					
Expansion/abandonment	X					X	X	
Budgeting	X						X	X
Acquisitions/divestiture	X					X	X	
Cost reduction	X	X	X	X	X		X	
Order profitability	X	X	X				X	X

represent a charge against earnings, and managers responsible for profits carefully scrutinize and challenge them. Because they are traceable, they are controllable. They are a powerful force for reducing overhead costs that would otherwise never be scrutinized by someone with a direct profit responsibility.

Advantages of Tracing

Unlike the cross-subsidization of allocations based on companywide overhead rates, the tracing of activities to users on the basis of usage will distinguish between intensive users and light users of activities. Compare the impact of tracing the invoicing activity. In traditional accounting, the costs associated with issuing an invoice are allocated to products on a volume-related basis such as direct labor, machine hours, or total division gross revenues. In activity accounting, the costs would be traced by usage.

By the traditional method a division selling to thousands of small-volume retail customers—the division that probably causes the need to allocate significant resources to the invoicing center—is charged too little invoicing cost while a division with a small number of high-volume industrial customers is overcharged for the invoicing activity.

Activity accounting militates against the misuse of resources that is usually associated with such cross-subsidized allocation. This gives activity managers incentive to keep their operations competitive by continually identifying and cost-effectively eliminating generators of waste.

How to Trace Costs

Costs are traced to the final cost objective through a bill of activities. A bill of activity (BOA) specifies the sequence of activities and the quantity of each activity consumed in achieving enterprise missions such as manufacturing a product, providing the manufacturing process, or servicing a customer.

The BOA includes *all* activities traceable to the final cost objective, such as development-related activities, operational activities, and support-related activities. In other words, the bill of activities manages all activities over the entire life cycle. Activities that are independent of a production order are charged on a per unit basis over the planned production volume of the product. A cost is computed by multiplying the activity quantity (as specified in the BOA) by the activity unit cost previously computed by the activity accounting system.

A typical bill of activities includes:

Activity	Life-Cycle Cost	Cost per Unit
Development		
Product design	X	X
Manufacturing process design	X	X
Quality planning	X	X
Manufacturing		
Manufacturing process 1		X
Set-up		X
Material movement		X
Material storage		X
Manufacturing process 2		X
Logistics and support		
Shipping		X
Logistics	X	X
Field support	X	X

The primary functions of a BOA include the following:

1. A bill of activities separates the quantity of an activity from the cost of the activity. A bill of activities specifies the sequence and quantity of activities. The cost of an activity is separately computed by the activity accounting system. This approach simplifies the standard-setting process because the BOA need only to be modified if there is a change to the activity/process. Changes to the cost of the factors of production *do not* require a modification to the BOA.
2. A bill of activities facilitates a mix of different cost behavior patterns without the need to choose a single allocation basis. Each activity in a BOA is separate and distinct. Therefore, each activity with a unique cost behavior pattern will have a different activity measure. (See the figure on the following page.)

COST PRECISION

The precision of a product cost depends on accurate knowledge of future business conditions including the production volume or the number of years a product, technology, or other asset will be used. Such precise knowledge of the future is impossible. As a result an activity cost must be based on estimates and is necessarily imprecise. However, it is erroneous to assume that because activity costs are based on imprecise estimates, the information is not useful to managers. Estimates derived from realistic cost behavior patterns provide an excellent basis for making routine decisions and control-

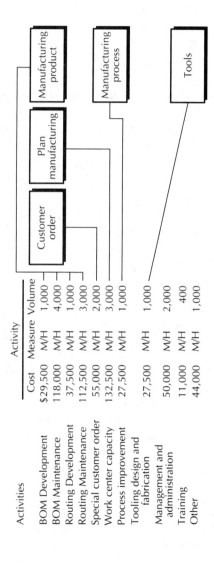

ling manufacturing operations. These cost behavior patterns and estimated costs form the foundation for calculating product cost.

The issue of cost precision rests on three primary criteria:

- Consistency of cost and planning system
- Error tolerance
- Cost versus benefit of accurate information

Consistency of Cost and Planning System

For information to be of value to a decision maker, the information and the decision criteria must be consistent. For example, consider the investment decision to purchase a five-axis spar machine. The investment decision requires forecasts from the product manager, manufacturing engineers, production schedulers, and others about the type and volume of parts to be processed on the new NC machine during its anticipated useful life. The return on investment for the new machine was predicated on these assumptions and expectations. If the cost accounting department decides to use time-basis depreciation, the reported cost will bear no relationship to the assumptions used to justify the investment.

Skeptics might ask, "So what?" The investment and cost systems are separate and distinct. They would be correct if the goal of cost accounting is to report a product cost in accordance with external requirements. However, if the goal of the cost accounting system is to provide information that can be used to manage cost, then the analysis of deviations between actual operations and the investment plan provides a basis for implementing corrective action. If the actual level of production, for example, was significantly below the forecasted production used in the investment analysis, then the technology component of cost will exceed target. Knowledge of this situation early in the life cycle of the five-axis mill will enable management to take corrective action such as redesigning products to use the mill.

Viewed from the myopic perspective of cost precision, time-based depreciation is superior. Viewed from the perspective of value to the decision maker, volume-based depreciation is superior.

Error Tolerance

Decision support systems are far less tolerant of certain types of errors than others. For example, bills of material accuracy in an MRP system is more critical than inventory record accuracy. An inventory record error might be on the plus side, or there might still be enough material for immediate requirements even though there is not as much material as the records show. But a bill of materials error is usually significant in that it either calls out the wrong component or omits a component.

The error tolerance of an activity accounting system is normally not an inhibitor to the achievement of value from the system. Consider an activity analysis that specifies 15 hours of assembly. When the assembly is completed, 15 hours will be credited against the plan. Even if the standard is off and the assembly activity really took 18 hours, 15 hours were planned and 15 hours were credited. The 3-hour difference is most likely due to an efficiency variance at the activity level.

If an activity standard is wrong, then the earned hours when compared with actual hours show a significant variance that would be investigated. Thus there is considerable tolerance in the accuracy of the standards required in a cost management system. Obviously, if the standards are biased in any given direction, output will tend to be higher or lower than planned over a period of time. Nevertheless, the cost management system itself does not require precision in the activity standards.

Cost Versus Benefit of Accurate Information

A third important criterion to consider is the cost versus the benefit of the accuracy of the information. Although the only theoretically correct procedure is that which is based on the most accurate information, the cost associated with obtaining this precision often exceeds the value to the decision maker. Thus the use of surrogate bases often provides an acceptable level of precision with a significant reduction in accounting for costs. Once a planned activity cost is determined, it should be used throughout the year. The planned cost will remain unchanged until the planning assumptions change.

COST SIGNIFICANCE

The significance of a cost is important in determining the precision required. The use of Pareto's Law (80/20 rule) is critical in determining significance. Typically, 80 percent of an enterprise's activities are consumed in producing 20 percent of the outputs of the activity. The idea behind the 80/20 rule of thumb is to focus the planning and control resources on the significant activities. Surrogates are used for other activities that have much less demonstrable effect on cost and performance.

The flexibility of the bill of activities approach permits the cost management system to determine a product cost for a single product. It is a common practice initially to determine a product cost for only "A" items (top 80 percent of revenue generators) and not for all products/components. This approach is a practical method of starting and operating a cost management system without having to wait for all the components to be properly costed. The number of significant errors due to erroneous product cost is likely to be quite low.

The use of surrogates early in the cost management development stage does not imply that accurate information should never be collected. What is proposed is that as more accurate information becomes available as a by-product of computerization, surrogates can be replaced with more accurate causal factors.

SUMMARY

Traditional methods of cost accounting are based on a product focus in the belief that all resources are acquired to support the manufacturing process. As a consequence, costs are considered to be direct or indirect to products.

Activity accounting focuses on the cost of activities. Product cost becomes a secondary objective. In other words, once the cost of an activity is known, it can be related to any cost objective—a customer, channel of distribution, or product. The process of identifying and quantifying the specific activities in the final cost objective is known as tracing. Because traceable costs are controllable, traceability facilitates management control.

Costs are traced to a final cost objective through a bill of activities, which specifies the sequence of activities and the amount of each activity consumed.

10

ACTIVITY PRODUCT COST

The purpose of this chapter is to:

- Contrast the differences between traditional and activity accounting–based product cost
- Describe the conventional approach to product cost, including its limitations
- Describe an activity accounting approach to product cost, including an in-depth discussion of the cost elements that are traceable
- Discuss special considerations such as:
  - Product cost calculation frequency
  - Set-up costs
  - Bottleneck costs
  - Work orders

In activity accounting, resources are consumed in the execution of activities. Products consume activities and materials. An activity product cost system assigns materials and all traceable activities to products based on the usage of each activity. Activity accounting represents a major change from traditional cost accounting. The primary differences include the following:

- Emphasis is on determining the cost of the manufacturing and support activities (processes). Product cost is a secondary cost objective.
- Direct labor is charged to the activity (process) rather than the product. This approach eliminates the need to voucher the labor to products except in cases where the accuracy is suspect because of the variability and magnitude of the estimated labor content.
- A cost pool is synonymous with an activity. The practice of using a single or limited number of cost pools is eliminated.
- Activity usage is based on the number of activity measures consumed by the product. An activity measure is the output of the activity.
- The direct tracing of activities to products reduces the amount of overhead to be allocated to products.

- The direct tracing of activities to products does not distinguish between direct or indirect costs. The cost is directly assigned where a cause-and-effect relationship can be established between the activity and the product. Traceable costs such as marketing, sales, engineering, and other support costs are directly charged to products. This approach results in a focus on total company cost, not just manufacturing cost.

- **Product cost** includes the total cost to design, manufacture, and distribute a product. Many life-cycle costs, which have traditionally been expensed, will be traced to the product and distributed over its life. Life-cycle cost provides management with an understanding of long-term profitability, allows better matching of pricing strategies to product cost at different life-cycle stages, and makes possible the quantification of the cost impact of process and product design choices.

- The impact of changes in the volume of activities on product cost is determined.

- Nonfinancial performance measures are incorporated to judge product performance.

The two primary benefits of activity accounting are that it provides a company with (1) an accurate product cost and (2) visibility of cost reduction and performance improvement opportunities. Competition increases the need for an accurate product cost because a company can't pass on inefficiencies through higher prices. Accurate and detailed information on the actual production cost is vital in pricing, vendor selection, make/buy, design to cost, and similar decisions. Perhaps even more important than knowing product cost is having visibility of waste and cost reduction and performance improvement opportunities to enable management to increase competitiveness.

USES OF PRODUCT COST

An accurate determination of product cost is important because a large number of business decisions use product cost data. To be relevant the reported product cost must mirror the manufacturing process.

Product cost information is required in various forms and at different levels of detail to meet objectives such as the following:

- Establishing selling prices
- Estimating product cost for new products and special one-time orders

- Determining the profitability for expansion or abandonment of different business segments, such as product lines, market segments, distribution channels, or customers
- Calculating the **gross margins** associated with individual products
- Facilitating make/buy decisions on whether to manufacture a part internally or purchase it from an outside vendor
- Assisting in the investment analysis process
- Valuing inventory and calculating cost of goods sold for external financial reporting purposes
- Assisting in off-shore sourcing decisions

TRADITIONAL APPROACH TO PRODUCT COST

The product cost model implemented in most factories identifies three major elements in the cost of a manufactured product:

- **Direct materials:** The acquisition costs of all materials that are identified as a part of the finished goods and can be traced to the finished goods in an economically feasible manner.
- **Direct labor:** The wages of all labor that can be associated with production in an economically feasible manner.
- **Factory overhead:** All costs other than direct labor and direct materials that are associated with the manufacturing process. Factory overhead is considered an indirect cost and cannot be traced directly to specific jobs or units. An overhead application rate is used to assign a reasonable portion of factory overhead costs to products. The essence of overhead allocation is the top-down application of costs from a cost center to *all* products manufactured during the period.

The diagram on the next page illustrates the basic flow of costs in a traditional cost accounting system.

To illustrate this approach, consider the manufacture of two products with equal production volume.

Step 1

Labor and materials are assigned directly to each product where feasible. Direct labor and material costs are easily attached to products. Material

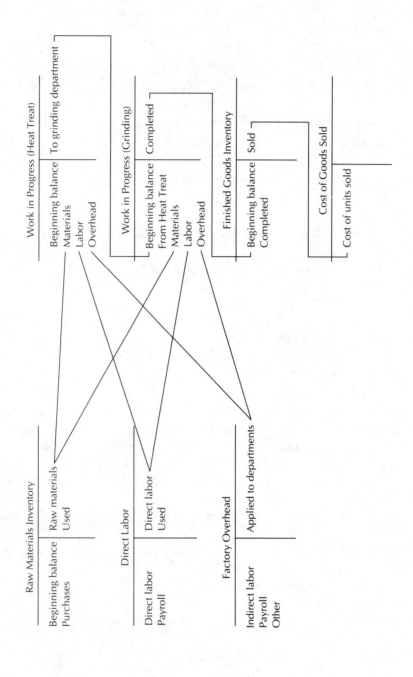

charges are posted from material requisitions and direct labor charges from time tickets.

	Products		
	A	B	Total
Annual Cost (in $1000s)	$	$	$
Direct labor			
Direct labor wages	3,000	1,000	4,000
Direct materials			
Raw materials	3,000	3,000	6,000
Purchased components	500	500	1,000
Total	$3,500	$3,500	$7,000

Step 2

All remaining costs are considered overhead and applied to products on a predetermined basis. Overhead is typically applied to products according to an overhead rate computed by dividing overhead costs by a rate base such as direct labor hours or cost, materials, and machine hours. An overhead application rate expresses a relationship of factory overhead to a factor of production that can be traced directly to products. Factory overhead is assigned to products in proportion to this factor.

The following procedures are used to apply overhead to products:

Determine costs to be included in overhead: Factory overhead typically includes all costs other than direct costs and selling, general, and administrative (SG&A).

Determine the period of benefit: Two rules of thumb for determining whether a cost should be capitalized are:

- Costs that benefit current production should be expensed.
- If the future benefit is uncertain, the costs should be expensed.

The decision to capitalize or expense a cost centers upon whether the venture is expected to be successful and the future earnings are expected to be sufficient to match the known expenses. Expenditures that benefit multiple periods should be capitalized and charged to future periods as consumed or based on estimates of the portion of the asset that is applicable to the current period.

An example of a factory overhead budget:

Cost Category	$
Fringe benefits	4,000
Indirect labor wages	2,000
Production supplies	1,000
Material management	1,000
Utilities	750
Overtime premium	500
Administration and accounting	400
Depreciation	300
Shift premium	300
Data processing	250
Quality assurance	100
Plant supervision and management	275
Personnel	200
Scrap material	200
Taxes and insurance	150
Rework labor	150
Tools	100
Miscellaneous	100
Supplies/blueprint	200
Manufacturing engineering	400
R&D	1,000
Supervisory salary	225
Purchasing	50
Personnel	200
Data processing	225
Depreciation	100
Insurance	25
Utilities	30
Taxes	15
Total overhead	$14,245

Determine level of overhead control: Cost centers represent the smallest area of responsibility for which costs are accumulated. Typically, cost centers correspond to departments.

Select an allocation base and calculate an overhead rate: An overhead rate expresses the relationship of factory overhead to the selected base. Overhead charged to products according to machine hours, for example, assumes that the overhead cost component varies in proportion to machine hours. The procedure of calculating an overhead rate also assumes that budgeted overhead is a good approximation of actual overhead. As long as the actual total overhead cost and base rate approximate the forecasted volumes, the under/overabsorption of cost is minimal.

Accounting practice does not dictate criteria for choosing a basis of allocation, thus allowing companies significant latitude in their choice of allocation basis. The selection of direct labor, as an allocation basis, for example, is based on the assumption that a strong relationship exists between the amount of labor used to build the product and overhead. Jobs that require more direct labor generally require more indirect labor (supervision and time keeping), more wear and tear on machinery (depreciation), and greater use of utilities.

An overhead rate is computed as follows:

$$\frac{\text{Factory}}{\text{overhead}} = \frac{\text{Manufacturing overhead}}{\text{Direct labor}} = \frac{\$14,245}{\$\ 4,000} = 356\%$$

This results in the following overhead application:

	Products		
Annual Cost (in $1000s)	A	B	C
Factory overhead	$10,680	$3,565	$14,245

Step 3

Selling, general, administration (SG&A) costs are not part of manufacturing costs. SG&A represents a cost that benefits the entire enterprise and is not assigned to individual products. Selling costs are expenses incurred in marketing a product, including salespeople's salaries, commissions, and expenses; advertising; sales department salaries and expenses; and samples. General and administrative costs include the cost of managing or directing an enterprise, including management, public relations, and legal department. Generally accepted accounting principles dictate that these costs be expensed in the same period in which they are incurred and not be included in inventory. They are shown as a separate and distinct division in a profit-and-loss statement.

Examples of SG&A expenses include:

	$
Executives	750
Administration and accounting	400
Sales and marketing	300
Interest expense	100
Total SG&A	$1,550

Applying the traditional cost accounting model results in the following cost breakdown:

	Products		
	A $	B $	Total $
Direct labor	$ 3,000	$ 1,000	$ 4,000
Direct material	3,500	3,500	7,000
Overhead	10,680	3,565	14,245
Total product cost	17,180	8,065	25,245
SG&A			1,550
Total cost			$26,795

SHORTCOMINGS OF THE TRADITIONAL PRODUCT COST MODEL

The traditional product cost model distorts product cost for several reasons:

1. Factory overhead costs are allocated rather than traced to products.
2. The total overhead component of product cost has historically grown faster than direct costs. As overhead becomes a larger percentage of product cost, the distortion inherent in the allocation process causes the total product cost to increase.
3. Generally accepted accounting principles often dictate or influence cost accounting practices. One of these principles—the conservatism principle—is inconsistent with accurate product cost determination in two important ways:
    3a. The conservatism principle requires that reported cost be based on precise and easily verifiable data, whereas management often needs costs that are based on forecasts and plans.
    3b. The conservatism principle encourages expensing many costs in the current period that should be capitalized. This practice distorts life-cycle costs.
4. Many activities included in SG&A are traceable to specific products.

Each of these issues is discussed in more depth in the remainder of this section.

1. Factory Overhead Costs Are Allocated Rather Than Traced to Products

Factory overhead includes all costs other than direct labor and materials that are associated with the manufacturing process. Overhead is allocated from cost centers to products according to an overhead application rate. Whether a cost is allocated or traced depends on whether a cause-and-effect relationship is established.

For example, a common method of allocating purchasing costs to products is to include these costs in a materials overhead and charge them to products on the basis of material cost. These costs are allocated because a direct cause-and-effect relationship cannot be established between purchasing costs and individual products—so a surrogate, material cost, is used.

On the other hand, purchasing costs can be traced to products by identifying the cause-and-effect relationship between purchasing activities and products. Consider the activity of ordering material. The number of purchase orders (the output of the activity of ordering material) can be traced to products based on the number of purchase orders consumed. The number of purchase orders necessary to acquire the material for any production order can be precisely specified—that is, a cause-and-effect relationship can be established and the cost of ordering material can be directly traced to products rather than allocated. For example, if the purchasing department processed 6,000 purchase orders during the year, and a complex product required 25 purchase orders, $625 (25 purchase orders at $25 per purchase order) is traceable to the product.

Under **responsibility accounting**, costs are assigned to managers of each organizational unit responsible for a set of related but unique activities. These costs are homogeneous with respect to function, but each activity has its own unique cost behavior pattern. The composite cost is therefore, a mixture of several cost behaviors. For example, consider a procurement department:

Cost Center: Procurement Department

Account	Description	Actual $	Budget $	Variance $
0009	Wages and salaries, salaried	80,150	83,000	2,850
0010	Wages and salaries, hourly	124,360	110,000	(14,360)
0201	Benefits, salaried	21,812	22,600	788
0202	Benefits, hourly	37,688	32,600	(5,088)
0352	Travel	62,515	70,500	7,985
0366	Facilities	32,000	32,000	0
0380	Supplies	1,394	1,500	106
0463	Training	20,240	30,000	9,760
	Total	$380,159	$382,200	$ 2,041

The purchasing department is responsible for procurement planning, vendor selection/evaluation, vendor negotiation, purchase orders, and vendor coordination. The resources consumed in each activity, the cost behavioral pattern, and cost drivers for each activity would be unique. Consider first the resources consumed in each activity:

Activity Description	Actual $	Budget $	Variance $
Procurement planning	29,150	30,000	850
Vendor selection and evaluation	43,360	45,200	1,840
Vendor negotiation	45,632	50,000	4,368
Order material	161,492	150,000	11,492
Vendor coordination	100,525	107,000	6,475
Total	$380,159	$382,200	$2,041

The department spends $161,492 (42 percent) on the purchase order activity and $29,150 (8 percent) on procurement planning.

Next consider the cost behavior patterns and the activity measures of the activities. Vendor negotiation, for example, varies with the number of new vendors; ordering material, on the other hand, varies with the number of purchase orders or purchase order lines.

Finally, consider the cost drivers. The principal cost drivers for vendor negotiation include vendor policy (multiple vendors or sole source) and degree of product standardization. The principal cost drivers for purchase orders include order size, purchasing policy, stocking policy (JIT or material stocking), and degree of product standardization.

Traditional cost systems muddle unique activities by capturing cost at the cost element level rather than by activities. This *systematically* distorts the cost of individual products by including a mixture of activities with different cost behavior patterns. For example, knowing the procurement department spends $124,360 on salaries does not provide any insight into how the salaries are being employed. Thus costs must be allocated to products.

When costs are allocated, a product containing more direct labor hours (or material dollars, machine hours, and so on) than another product is assumed to incur proportionately more indirect cost. Volume-related allocations reliably distribute overhead costs to products only if overhead varies directly with volume output.

By decomposing cost elements into unique activities, costs are traced through the manufacturing activities to products rather than being allocated.

Costs are traceable if a cause-and-effect relationship is established between the activity and the manufacturing process. Costs are allocated if no cause-and-effect relationship is established.

Consider the development of a process plan for a new product. The number of hours expended by the manufacturing engineer to develop the routing is directly attributable to the product. Failure to trace costs to products and processes causes companies to resort to allocating costs on an arbitrary basis with a resulting cost distortion.

2. The Total Overhead Component of Product Cost Has Historically Grown Faster than Direct Cost

Today, indirect cost has become a significant component of manufacturing cost. In the past environment, where direct labor and material were the predominant factors of production and overhead costs were nominal, the product cost distortion caused by improper selection of an overhead allocation method was minimal. The concept of materiality dominated.

The rapid increase in overhead costs lies at the heart of this distortion, which is exacerbated by the use of direct labor, the *replaced* component of product costs, as the allocation basis. As companies have increasingly incorporated information systems and automation into the manufacturing enterprise, the overhead category, rather than labor or material, has grown at the fastest pace. Traditional systems consider this category fixed in the short and medium run, yet instead it has been the most dynamic.

Because overhead is a significant component of product cost, the choice of allocation methods has a major impact on product cost. Consider a manufacturer who is evaluating labor hours and machine hours as a basis to allocate overhead. Depending on which of the two methods is selected, a substantial difference in the amount of cost applied to the product would result.

Assume:

	Product A $	Product B $
Labor (24 hours at $10)	40	200
Material	300	300
Technology (12 hours at $20)	200 (10 hours)	40 (2 hours)
Other overhead	385	385
Total	$925	$925

To illustrate the importance of choosing an appropriate basis of allocation, let us first compute a product cost by direct labor. An overhead rate is computed as follows:

$$\frac{\text{Overhead}}{\text{calculation}} = \frac{\text{Total cost} - \text{Direct labor and material}}{\text{Total direct labor cost}}$$

$$= \frac{\$1,010}{\$240} = 421 \text{ percent}$$

The accounting system calculates a product cost by the machine hour–based overhead rate as follows:

	Product A $	Product B $
Direct labor	40	200
Direct material	300	300
Overhead	168	842
Total product cost	$580	$1342

Next consider computing a product cost by machine hour:

$$\frac{\text{Overhead}}{\text{calculation}} = \frac{\text{Total cost} - \text{Direct labor and material}}{\text{Total machine hours}}$$

$$= \frac{\$1010}{12} = \$84.17 \text{ per hour}$$

The accounting system calculates a product cost by the labor-based overhead rate as follows:

	Product A $	Product B $
Direct labor	40	200
Direct material	300	300
Overhead	842 (10 hours)	168 (2 hours)
Total product cost	$1,182	$668

This example illustrates how selection of an allocation basis dramatically impacts cost when overhead becomes a significant proportion of total cost.

For illustrative purposes, assume the average difference between allocation methods is 40 percent. If the overhead component of total cost is 10
percent, then the 40 percent discrepancy in the choice of overhead methods
results in only a 4 percent difference in total cost (40 percent × 10 percent). On the other hand, if the total overhead consists of 40 percent of total
product cost, then a difference of 16 percent in total cost (40 percent × 40
percent) results. As overhead costs increase in magnitude, the importance
of selecting allocation methods based on economic consequence increases.

3a. The Conservatism Principle Requires that Reported Cost be Based on Precise and Easily Verifiable Data

To accurately match overhead costs to products requires precise knowledge
of future business conditions including production volumes. Such precise
knowledge of the future is impossible. As a result, the matching of overhead
cost to products must be based on estimates and is necessarily imprecise.
An ingrained fear of making decisions on imprecise data causes companies
to resort to using allocation bases that are easily verifiable but irrelevant.

To illustrate this point consider recent surveys (including a 1987
NAA/CAM-I study) that demonstrate that the prevalent practice in U.S.
industry is to use direct labor–based allocation and straight line depreciation in spite of the fact that these practices are increasingly less reflective
of manufacturing reality. The reason that they are popular is that both direct
labor–based allocation and straight line depreciation use data that are easily
verified and understandable. However, the reported cost is not relevant to
decision making because the assumptions underlying the approaches are not
valid.

It is important to base cost decisions on relevant information even if the
data is based on imprecise estimates. Estimates derived from realistic cost
behavior patterns provide an excellent basis for making routine decisions
and controlling manufacturing operations. Consider machine hour–based
depreciation. The company must estimate the number of hours of usage for
the machine per year and in total for the life of the machine. Clearly this
type of estimating is much less precise than merely estimating the number of
years the machine will be used and recovering the cost in equal increments
during its period of usefulness.

However, consider the cost behavior patterns of a machine. First, rarely
is the usage of the machine steady throughout its life. As the product demands fluctuate, so will machine usage. A depreciation method not based
on machine hours charges too much depreciation during periods of low
demand and conversely too little cost during periods of high demand.

Second, the only direct relationship between machine cost and products is in machine hours. This relationship is analogous to that of direct labor and products. The amount of time a machine processes specific products varies by product. A company is forced to use surrogates such as labor hours or material cost, which rarely reflect how much machine cost is consumed in manufacturing products.

3b. The Conservatism Principle Encourages Expensing Many Costs in the Current Period That Should Be Capitalized

The primary reasons that companies expense costs of activities that benefit future periods are that this course of action is conservative, minimizes taxable income, and maximizes cash flow. If start-up costs are capitalized and the product, system, or investment is abandoned or unprofitable, then a company must write off the asset. It is believed that a company is financially healthier by expensing costs that are potentially risky.

There are several problems with expensing rather than capitalizing the cost of activities that benefit future periods. First, any potentially traceable costs that are treated as an expense in the current period rather than matched to products result in product cost distortion.

Cost distortion occurs because of the following:

- The magnitude of cost is large. When one considers the many engineering, R&D, and marketing activities that are necessary to commercialize a product or implement an investment, a great number of costs are evident. They are needed if an enterprise is to remain in business in the long run.
- The expenditure pattern is uneven. The distribution of activities between those that benefit the current or future periods varies based on factors such as management policy and budgetary considerations.

Second, expensing confuses the issue of matching and risk. The goal of matching is to infer how costs attach to products. Risk is a function of the probability of achieving the desired results. Risk is directly related to anticipated variability of estimates.

The issues of risk and matching are separate and distinct. No matter what the degree of risk, the identification of how costs attach to products is unchanged. Risk should be managed through a rigorous review of all activities from start-up to retirement as events unfold in relation to the original plan. Risk should not be managed by the choice of accounting methods.

Third, product life cycles are decreasing. Shorter product life cycles increase the need to understand the total product cost over its entire life cycle to determine profitability. Reduced life cycles mean companies have less available time to respond to changes in market demand and to recover product/process development costs.

4. Many Activities Included in SG&A Are Traceable to Specific Products

Consider advertising. General company advertising benefits all products and is not traceable to individual products. Specific product advertising is traceable to individual products. Although there is a spin-off effect to other products, the primary goal of specific product advertising is to increase the sales of the product being advertised. Failure to trace costs misrepresents the profitability of the products. Similarly, sales commissions are often product-dependent and thus traceable to specific products. Again, failure to trace these costs distorts product cost.

IMPLICATIONS OF PRODUCT COST DISTORTION

Product distortion leads to cross-subsidization of products. When used to guide marketing strategies, distorted cost information encourages managers to produce many low-volume product lines. The results, in many cases, are declining profit margins and perceived difficulty competing with focused (usually foreign) competitors.

Product variety and complexity increase cost distortion. Several factors have contributed to the growth of overhead in recent decades. The primary ones include increased diversity, or scope, of output (not increased volume, or scale, of output), increased use of technology, and increased regulations. Thus traditional cost accounting systems tend to overcost high-volume products—not the ones that cause most growth in overhead—and undercost the low-volume products that are chiefly responsible for the overhead growth.

Many overhead costs are driven by diversity—volume, product, process and customer—which increases the complexity of the production process. Activities such as material movement, scheduling, and set-ups tend to grow with the number of products in the product line and the support required in complex production environments. If a plant produces only one product with no options, the scheduling function is a simple task; complexities (and the requirement for additional scheduling personnel and costs) occur because of the variety of products, sizes, colors, and options produced.

The conventional methodology of allocating the cost of overhead activities related to product variety and complexity on a volume-related basis distorts product cost.

ACTIVITY PRODUCT COST

Activity accounting is based on the principle that activities consume resources whereas products consume activities and materials. Product costing is enhanced by more specific tracing of support costs that have traditionally been lumped in overhead and allocated to all products. Activity product cost is derived by identifying the materials and activities necessary to build a product and determining the quantity of activity for each product. Product cost is determined by summing the costs of all traceable activities.

Consider the manufacture of a bearing. The part routing specifies the following operations:

- Turning
- Heat treating
- Grinding
- Honing
- Assembly

When the cost of each activity required to manufacture a bearing has been determined the manufacturing component of product cost can be computed. The cost of turning, for example, consists of the cost of direct labor, the turning machine, and the material consumed in the turning operation. Labor is specified by the routing; material is specified by the bill of material; technology is specified in the routing.

The factors of production are easily associated with each activity; the cost of the manufacturing process is directly computed from the amount of the turning activity the product consumes. The manufacturing component of cost for the bearing is the sum of the cost of its activities.

However, to concentrate exclusively on these prime manufacturing costs excludes the many activities that are required to support the manufacture of a product: The product must be designed; the labor, machines, facilities, and material must be procured; the manufacturing process must be scheduled and controlled; performance must be reported to internal and external parties; and a myriad of other support activities must be accomplished. Each of these activities consumes resources and is a prerequisite for production.

Support activities have traditionally been included in overhead and allocated to products on a direct basis such as direct labor, machine hours, or materials. In activity accounting there is no need to allocate support activities that are *traceable* to products. Consider the product design activity. A product cannot be manufactured without being designed. The product design activity is easily identifiable with a specific product; one need not lump engineering costs in overhead and allocate the costs to all products. Failure to trace costs distorts product cost.

To further illustrate the importance of tracing activities to products let us consider the major activities of a typical material control department. They include the following:

- Incoming material handling
- In-process material handling
- Outgoing material handling
- Raw material storage
- WIP storage
- Finished goods storage
- Management and administration
- Training
- Other

Material-handling activities are controlled differently from the activities of material storage. The costs of material handling attach to the products being moved. Products might or might not be stored depending on their routing. Only products that require storage should be charged with the cost of material storage. To include material storage costs in overhead and arbitrarily allocate them to all products penalizes products that use flow lines.

An activity cost is the sum of the factors of production (natural expense categories) and intercompany activities. Determining an activity product cost involves the following process:

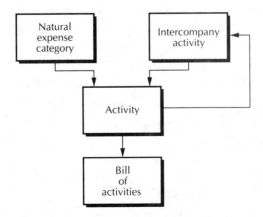

Activity accounting systems compute a product cost by tracing all product-related activities to products on the basis of the products' usage of each activity. For example, quality costs would be assigned where the quality effort is expended, and taxes and utilities would be assigned on occupied square footage. A product cost becomes a summation of the cost of all traceable activities to design, manufacture, and distribute a product. Activities represent the capabilities of a manufacturing enterprise. The manufacture of a product uses varying amounts of those capabilities. A product consumes activities during its life cycle—R&D, design, plan manufacturing, manufacture, sale, delivery, and service. For example, one state-of-the-art product may require a significant amount of R&D and design activities. Another commodity-type product would require fewer of these activities.

Many support functions such as production supervision and quality control involve product-related activities. From interviews, the percentage of time spent on activities is determined and traced according to the number of transactions. When the interview has not identified specific measures for activities, a general measure such as the number of production hours per product is used.

Administrative support activities cannot be directly related to specific products or equipment. These activities relate to the people managed or supported. Activities of personnel, plant managers, and secretaries have many administrative aspects that are nontraceable and must be allocated to products.

An activity accounting system better mirrors the manufacturing process and therefore distorts product cost less than the traditional model for the following reasons:

- Activities represent the lowest level of homogeneous cost.
- There are multiple bases of assignment inherent in the selection of activity measures.
- Activities facilitate the linking of related activities (business process), which transcends organizational boundaries. This group of cost can then be assigned en masse to the originating cause.
- Most variances are caused by the process rather than the product.
- Life cycle permits better matching of time periods.
- Today only two major classifications of cost exist—product and SG&A. In activity accounting there can be others, such as orders.
- It is possible to trace all product-related costs including SG&A.
- There is minimal dependence for accurate activity costs on a company's existing organizational structure and level of detail captured within the accounting system.

ACTIVITY PRODUCT COST APPROACH

Product Bill of Activities

The traceability of product cost can be improved by identifying all significant activities triggered by the decision to build a product. The activities are
subsets to the manufacturing process summarized in the statement, "Make
product." One approach is to specify this process in terms of a bill of activity (BOA) based on the sequence of activities. The BOA includes *all*
business activities, both support and production, required to manufacture a
product.

The BOA activity approach provides management with the capability of
defining the quantity and cost of activities within a product, across product
families, or within the entire enterprise.

A bill of activity is created in two steps:

- *Step 1:* Determine costed bill of activities for business processes. Key
  business processes that are consumed in a product are costed in total
  rather than listed individually.
- *Step 2:* Determine costed bill of activities for products.

Activity	Activity Measure	Activity Quantity	Activity Cost $	Life Cycle Cost 5,000 Units	Current Unit Cost
Product engineering	Hours	1,000	50	50,000	$10
Process planning	Hours	375	40	13,500	3
Material acquisition		10	15		150
Manufacturing activity 1	Inserts	500	10		50
Manufacturing activity 2	Machine hours	5	60		300
Manufacturing activity 3	Burn-in hours	8	8		64
Manufacturing activity 4	Man hours	20	15		300
Packaging	Cubic feet	4	7		28
Shipping	Pounds	20	6		120

The source for determining the production activities of a product cost
is the parts process plan (routing). The routing specifies how a product is
built. The typical information available on most routings includes:

- Operation
- Department performing the operation

- Set-up hours per lot
- Labor grade for direct labor
- Direct labor hours per piece
- Machine type
- Machine hours
- Production lead time for move, queue, set-up, and run time for a typical lot

It is essential that the routing represents the way the order actually moves through the factory and the manufacturing processes. If it doesn't, the wrong activities will be charged against the product. When an alternate routing is used, the bill of activities for the order should reflect the alternate routing.

A product cost bill of activities represents all the activities necessary to manufacture a product. The bill of activities represents all activities over the entire life cycle. Activities that are independent of a production order are charged on a per unit basis over the planned production volume of the product.

A typical bill of activities includes:

Activity	Life-Cycle Cost	Cost per Unit
Product design	X	X
Manufacturing process design	X	X
Quality planning	X	X
Manufacturing process 1		X
Set-up		X
Material movement		X
Material storage		X
Manufacturing process 2		X
Shipping		X
Logistics	X	X
Field support	X	X

The primary costs that comprise a product cost include material, direct labor, technology, quality, engineering, manufacturing engineering, R&D, material handling, marketing, production support, customer support, and finished goods distribution. Those cost elements are described in greater detail below.

Material Costs

Material costs are derived from the **bill of material (BOM)**. A BOM is an engineering document that defines the product from the design point of view by listing components of each assembly and subassembly. The BOM structure pertains to the way the product is structured, and the material flow in and out of each state of completion. Thus the BOM specifies not only the composition of a product but also the process stages in that product's manufacture. It defines product structure in terms of levels of manufacture, each of which represents a step in the manufacture of the product. A graphic representation of a BOM is shown in the following figure:

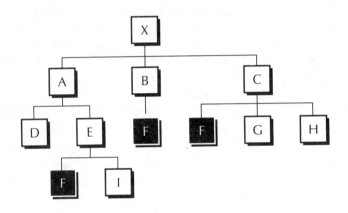

The BOM is the key source of material cost used to compute a product cost. Several activity product cost systems incorporate the BOM into the product cost roll-up, while others interface with the BOM and extract material cost in total. In determining a product cost, several features of the BOM are important:

1. A given component either can be purchased or internally manufactured. The cost of purchased material consists of the purchase price and all traceable costs of bringing the material to the activity that consumes it. The cost of a manufactured component consists of all traceable costs to produce the component.

2. A given component can exist in its own right as a uniquely identified physical unit (raw material, component part, subassembly) or as an already assembled component of another inventory item. In either case, the activities to build the component are identical. However, if the part is stored, the component cost will be higher due to the storage costs.

3. The BOM establishes the item lead times and timing of requirements. This information is used for performance measurement.

Direct Labor Costs

In a pure activity accounting system labor costs are charged to the manufacturing process and not to the individual products. The approach is based on the observation that laborers perform activities and products consume activities. Labor cost is one component of activity cost.

Labor costs are assigned to products according to the amount of the activity consumed by the product specified in the bill of activities. For example, the cost of the manual insertion activity is charged to the product according to the number of insertions specified in the product bill of activities. Based on the rates and number of operators assigned to an activity, a cost per activity measure is derived. For example, the labor associated with workers' manually inserting components in a board is charged to the manual insertion activity. Knowing the total number of manual inserts allows a company to compute a cost per manual insert.

There are several reasons for charging costs directly to activities rather than products. First, labor variances are more often the result of process variances than any aspect of the product. Demand changes (over or under), operator experience, and training variations result from operator efficiencies and inefficiencies. These factors cause variances related to activity rather than product. Second, labor reporting is greatly simplified because there is no need to voucher labor to products.

However, there are exceptions in which some labor-related costs require special time reporting. The primary situations include the following:

- *Estimates of direct labor are very imprecise.* It may be difficult to precisely estimate labor hours for one-time products.
- *Labor transferred between activities.* Determine if labor is being shifted between operations based on the complexity of the part.
- *Because of contractual requirement.* Defense regulations often require direct labor reports.
- *Floating labor.* Determine if additional laborers are hired to fill in for absent workers. Proper product costing requires accountability of the use of these workers.

Process variances for an activity are computed by comparing the labor hours earned during a time period with the actual hours expended. The earned hours are derived by summing the total hours specified in the bill for all products using the activity during the specified time period.

Continued significant variations between actual and earned hours might indicate that the product bills of activities must be reviewed. Those responsible for product profitability, such as the product/product line manager, should identify instances of above-normal activity. Those responsible for the process, such as the manufacturing manager, should identify instances of below-normal activity. Earned hours can be periodically validated by industrial engineering studies and random checks of actual time spent on parts as opposed to earned time.

Technology (Process) Costs

The costs of technology, or process, are traced to products on the basis of the usage of the activity as reflected in the activity measure (machine hours, and so on).

Quality Costs

Activities associated with quality are classified into four categories:

1. Prevention.

   Quality engineering
   Design and development of quality measurement and control equipment
   Calibration
   Training
   Administration of quality assurance system
   System audits
   Improvement projects

2. Appraisal.

   Laboratory acceptance testing
   Inspection and test
   Inspection and test set-up
   In-process inspection (not by inspectors)
   Product quality audits
   Review of inspection test results prior to acceptance
   Evaluation at customers' sites
   Data processing of inspection and test reports

3. Internal failure: Directly charged to department incurring cost but classified as a quality activity.

   Scrap
   Rework
   Troubleshooting
   Analysis of defects and failures

    Reinspection and retest
    Lost production due to supplier material
    Lost production due to own material
    Modification permits (contrary to process sheets)

4. External failures: Suggested activity measure is the number of returns from the field for poor quality. The source of information includes internal quality reports, vendor quality reports, and shipping reports.

    Complaints administration
    Reliability management: The engineering activity of tracking and analyzing customer returns to determine the causes of quality problems
    Product or customer service
    Product liability
    Product returns
    Product recalls
    Product replacement
    Marketing errors

Additional product-related costs include:

Warranty/service contract administration: The cost of warranty and service contract administration should be traced to the products according to the distribution of time and cost incurred in this activity. Additionally, warranty service costs should certainly be an element of the cost of quality report.

Field customer service: Field customer service activities include installations and repairs performed by the field service engineers. These costs should be charged to the specific product being repaired. The regional supervisor's cost and the cost of maintaining the field service offices would be factored into the activity rates used for charging the cost of these activities to segments. Repair work represents a cost of quality.

In-house repair: In-house repair activities include installations and repairs performed by the maintenance engineers. These costs should be charged to the specific product being repaired. The supervisor's cost and the cost of maintaining the repair office would be factored into the activity rates used for charging the cost of these activities to products. Repair work represents a cost of quality.

Engineering Costs

New product development: The costs related to developing new or enhanced products are charged directly to specific product/product lines. Engineering costs charged to specific projects/product lines by either the estimated number of engineering hours or a project-tracking system. Project-tracking systems can be manual time collection systems or can automatically extract from the CAD system. The source of the information includes payroll records and engineering and quality control reports. The costs of outside services, testing, and materials are directly charged to specific products through accounts payable.

Engineering changes/documentation control activities: These activities originate from design enhancement of products. Normally they are triggered by an engineering change order (ECO) and include control and administration of the following types of documentation:

- Marketing manuals
- Service manuals and specifications
- Installation manuals
- Bills of materials
- Routings

The cost of these activities should be traced to products according to the number of ECOs a product line generates. However, when these activities are performed for a new product under development, the costs should be directly assigned to the product on the basis of engineering hours.

Manufacturing Engineering Costs

Activities associated with manufacturing engineering include the following:

- Process planning
- Process modification
- NC programming

Manufacturing engineering activities represent a life-cycle cost that should be associated with the manufacturing process.

Research and Development (R&D) Costs

Activities associated with research and development include the following:

- Basic research
- Manufacturing process research

- New product development
- New manufacturing process development

Basic research and manufacturing process research should be charged to a companywide, nontraceable overhead or applied to development projects as a secondary activity, depending on company policy.

Material-Handling/Work-In-Progress Costs

The activity associated with material handling/work-in-progress is material movement, storage of material, and associated record keeping. Its costs are traced to the material-handling activity. Each product bill of activity would include a material-handling activity based on the part routing.

Market and Advertising Costs

Activities associated with marketing and advertising include the following:

Corporate sales: This includes the costs of the vice president of sales and other personnel who administer the sales organization and all associated support costs such as occupancy cost. Sales reporting is included in this function. The costs of the corporate sales function should be treated as a secondary activity within the sales department and allocated to the primary selling activities.

Sales administration: The personnel who are assigned to this activity support the field sales offices by performing order entry and customer service activities. These costs will be assigned to the activities performed and subsequently traced to products or orders.

Field sales: The total cost of each region's field sales efforts should be considered directly traceable to products.

Major account administration: The personnel assigned to this activity support selected major customers. The cost of the activity should be charged to the products supported.

Product management: The cost of managers dedicated to the support and management of individual product lines should be charged to the products supported.

- *Market research:* Activities related to companywide market research are treated as secondary activity and allocated to the department's primary activities. Research efforts for specific product lines should be charged to the product line through general ledger project numbers.

- *Trade shows:* The cost of trade shows for individual product lines should be charged to the product line through general ledger project numbers. If numerous products are exhibited at a show, the cost is treated as a secondary activity and allocated to the department's primary activities.
- *Media advertising:* The costs of product-specific newspaper or regional publication advertisements are assigned directly to products. Advertisements for numerous products or companywide advertisements are treated as nontraceable SG&A costs. In either case these costs are assigned to territories through a general ledger project number.
- *Sales literature:* The costs of brochures or literature developed for a single product are assigned to the product. Sales literature of a more general nature is treated as a nontraceable SG&A cost.
- *Administration:* Administrative costs are treated as a secondary activity and allocated to the department's primary activities.

Production Support Costs

Depending on the complexity of the product, significantly different production support activities can arise. The primary production support activities that can be assigned to products include the following:

- Scheduling
- Production control

Production support activities are traceable to orders and do not vary according to order quantity. Thus small lot size orders require a proportionally larger production support cost than large quantity orders.

Customer Technical Support Costs

In-house technical support people handle a variety of questions from end users and sales representatives. They also deal with customer returns. Their costs are directly traceable to product lines on the basis of the number of return authorizations generated during the quarter for each product. Where the analysis is unable to trace costs to the specific product/product lines supported, these costs are considered a common company cost. However, in product life-cycle costing all costs of this activity can be charged to specific products.

Finished Goods and Distribution Costs

Activities associated with finished goods and distribution include the following:

- Storing finished goods in the warehouse
- Transportation
- Packaging/shipping
- Field support
- Supplying spares
- Equipment maintenance
- Coordinating dealerships

These costs should be directly traceable to products/product lines through product bill of activities.

COST MANAGEMENT EXAMPLE

To illustrate the significance of tracing costs, consider the impact of tracing the following costs:

Traceable Labor	Annual cost $1000s
Direct labor and fringe benefits	4,500
Set-up	600
Rework	300
Overtime premium	250
Training	150
Shift premium	125
Workmans' compensation	75
Miscellaneous	50
Subtotal	6,050

Traceable Materials	$1000s
Raw materials	6,000
Purchased components	1,000
Production purchasing department	350
Shipping	225
Subtotal	7,575

Other Traceable Costs	$1000s
Tooling material and labor	1,700
Maintenance material and labor	800
Quality assurance	900
Material handling	800
Production utilities	500
Depreciation on equipment	300
Manufacturing engineering	400
Scrap	200
Product design engineering	600
WIP carrying cost	270
Industrial engineering	225
Product-specific advertising	50
Applied R&D	450
Production control	400
Subtotal	7,595

Nontraceable Costs	$1000s
Plant supervision and management	275
Building utilities	280
Plant security	75
Data processing	925
Building taxes and insurance	175
Depreciation on real estate	100
Miscellaneous supplies	600
Other purchasing	50
Other capital carrying costs	50
Miscellaneous	800
Subtotal	3,330

SG&A Costs	$1000s
Basic R&D	550
Administration	350
Marketing	250
Corporate personnel	840
Corporate data processing	750
Accounting	425
Subtotal	3,165

Total cost	$27,715

The new reported product cost would be calculated as follows:

	Products		
	A $	B $	Total $
Direct labor	4,695	1,565	6,260
Direct material	3,909	3,909	7,818
Direct technology	464	2,000	2,464
Quality	600	360	960
Engineering/R&D	1,000	2,033	3,033
WIP	100	41	141
Marketing and advertising	70	71	141
Production support	626	400	1,026
Finished goods and distribution	250	336	586
Nontraceable overhead	1,847	1,565	3,412
Total product cost	13,561	12,280	25,841
SG&A			1,874
Total cost			$27,715

Today the prime manufacturing costs include not only labor and material, but also technology.

	Products		
	A $	B $	Total $
Direct Labor			
Direct labor wages	3,000	1,000	4,000
Direct Materials			
Raw materials	3,000	3,000	6,000
Purchased components	500	500	1,000
Subtotal	3,500	3,500	7,000
Direct Technology	500	3,000	3,500
Total	$7,000	7,500	$14,500

SPECIAL CONSIDERATIONS

Product Cost Calculation Frequency

A bill of activities separates the quantity of an activity from the cost of the activity. A bill of activities specifies the sequence and quantity of activities. The cost of an activity is separately computed by the activity accounting system. This approach simplifies the standard-setting process because the

BOA need only be modified if there is a change to the activity/process. Changes to the cost of the factors of production do not require a modification to the BOA.

Set-up Costs

The conventional practice of manufacturing in lots in advance of current demand is intended to spread the set-up and ordering costs over a larger number of products and, as a consequence, to reduce the total annual cost of operation.

Set-up involves preparing a manufacturing process for operation for the first time. Set-up is dependent on the production schedule, the product complexity, and the manufacturing technology. If a process must be set up from scratch, a fixed amount of effort will be required. However, where the preceding process was set up for a part within the same family of parts, a changeover rather than an entire set-up is required. A **changeover** is a partial set-up in which not all procedures are required.

For example, to set up a punch press requires a major effort to change all the guides for different gauges, width, and material of coil stock. To change the guides requires a full set-up. However, only a minor effort is required to change from one die to another to make different items out of the same stock. This is a changeover. In packaging operations, there is frequently a major set-up effort for different bottle sizes, but minor effort to clean the machine for different liquids in the same type of bottle, and even smaller costs of changing language labels for the same product.

The cost of a set-up is often significant. An obvious cost is the time that it takes an operator to set up the machine to make the next part. Less obvious costs include the cost of paperwork associated with each set-up, the cost of inventory sitting idle during the set-up, and the scrap loss on the initial pieces. When operators are not experienced with a set-up, a learning curve occurs before the process is working at standard efficiency. Finally, when the machine is operating at full capacity, the productive time lost during a set-up increases cost.

Bottleneck Costs

Production bottlenecks are generally considered to be temporary blockages to increased output; they may occur anywhere in the production process. The stationary bottleneck is easy to identify because work in process accumulates behind it. Its cause is usually also clear—a machine has broken down, key workers are absent, or demand has outstripped the capacity of the process.

More subtle are bottlenecks that shift from one part of the process to another or have no clear cause. Inventories build up in different places at different times. Perhaps they result from flaws in a product's quality caused inadvertently by one or more workers trying to keep pace with production demands that should not have been placed on them. They may also be caused by missing parts, new product start-up, or changes in the mix of products through the factory. In such cases the remedies are less clear-cut.

A nebulous bottleneck situation is a chronic management dilemma of job shops and batch flow processes. In a batch flow (job shop) process capacity usage is volatile because the process flow is indeterminate. For example, a new order or product introduction changes the product mix and might place excessive demands on a single department.

Coming to a decision on how to remedy a bottleneck calls for an analysis of the cost associated with each option. Specifically, the analysis involves comparing the *extra* costs incurred by each alternative, because those were the only costs that differed between the options being considered.

The following example evaluates a set-up time reduction to highlight some of the problems with understanding the cost impact of bottlenecks. Suppose that two machines, A and B, support the same production activity. The time necessary for machine A to change from producing one product to producing another averages about 10 minutes, whereas the set-up time for machine B is 1 hour. An engineering study indicates that the set-up time of machine A could be reduced by half at a cost of $50,000; machine B's set-up time could also be cut in half at a cost of $5,000.

Superficially, machine B seems to pay off better in terms of time reduction per investment cost. This approach focuses on the work center at which the set-up reduction occurs by examining the cost savings in work center inventory and direct labor costs. However, this myopic view ignores the impact of the set-up reduction on subsequent operations and products.

When the impacts of a set-up time reduction are evaluated for the entire production system, the economics of the decision can alter dramatically. If, for example, machine A is set up 25 times a day, it can produce 1,000 units per day with its current changeover times. If machine B is set up 4 times a day, it can produce 1,500 units per day. As a consequence, the output of the production line is limited to the 1,000 units per day that machine A can produce.

Few benefits would be gained by reducing the set-up time on machine B because the output of the line would still be 1,000 units per day and no additional revenue would be generated. A small labor saving will result, but unless this saving reduces the number of employees or their time is redeployed to alternative activities, the cost saving is not realized. In most cases there are minimal benefits to reducing set-up time on a machine that is not creating a bottleneck.

Two substantial benefits can be realized by reducing the set-up time on machine A. First, the time saved increases plant capacity because machine A essentially controls the output of the factory. Alternatively, the additional time can be used to reduce the production lot sizes, thus increasing flexibility, or to expand the range of products to the line, both of which increase the effective variety of the factory output.

Benefits of a set-up time reduction should be examined in terms of capacity. If the set-up time of machine A is reduced to 5 minutes, the output of the machining activity will increase by 125 minutes per day; the 2 extra hours of activity capacity are worth a substantial sum of money. More throughput also decreases the overhead costs per unit. Seen another way, gains in capacity can offset reduced batch sizes, which in turn reduce work-in-progress inventory, increase response time, and improve customer service.

The cost accounting systems used in most firms are practically useless for this type of bottleneck decision. Estimating the benefits of reduced changeover time requires information other than the cost of machines and the hours saved. What is needed is an estimate of the value of increased capacity, variety, and flow times. Tracing the impact of the reduction to activities will better quantify the impacts of the decision.

Thus focusing on the work center may lead to an overestimation of the savings in set-up time reduction for machine B and an underestimation of the benefits of a set-up time reduction for machine A. Systemwide information is required for appropriate analysis. Such information must assess the effect of a set-up time reduction at a specific work center on the entire production process as well as the effect of such a reduction on product quality.

Profit Velocity

Profit velocity is the ratio of product profit to lead time.

$$\text{Profit velocity} = \frac{\text{Profit}}{\text{Lead time}}$$

Profit velocity is based on the observation that company profitability is a function of both the absolute profitability of a product and the number of products that can be produced during any given period of time. To illustrate profit velocity, consider two products:

Product	Profit $	Lead Time (Days)
A	50	5
B	35	2

Conventional cost accounting would proclaim product A more profitable than product B—which is correct in absolute terms. The profit velocity of the two products presents a different conclusion. The profit velocity for product A is $10 per production day while for product B it is $17.50 per production day. Assuming sufficient demand for product B, the company would be most profitable selling product B rather than product A.

Work Orders

Work orders should not be used for standard products—or for nonstandard products when the estimate is deemed sufficient. Work orders should be used when estimates might be considered suspect.

SUMMARY

An activity-based product cost is derived by tracing the usage of all activities necessary to build a product. A product cost becomes a summation of the cost of all traceable activities to design, procure material, manufacture, and distribute a product.

Activity accounting directly relates activities to the products that consume them. This is in contrast to the conventional cost accounting model, which spreads overhead costs among products on a basis that does not mirror their actual consumption. Product costing is enhanced by more specific tracing of support costs, which have traditionally been lumped into overhead and allocated to all products.

GLOSSARY

Abandonment analysis: The process of determining if it is more profitable to continue or discontinue a product or project.

Activity: A combination of people, technology, raw materials, methods, and environment that produces a given product or service. Activities describe what an enterprise does: the way time is spent and the outputs of the process. See *Process*.

Activity accounting: The collection of financial and operational performance information about significant activities of an enterprise.

Activity analysis: The breakdown of an enterprise into manageable segments for detailed analysis regarding cost and performance.

Activity dictionary: A listing of generic activities according to the functions performed by a typical company in an industry.

Activity management: The effective and consistent organization of an enterprise's activities.

Activity measure: A quantitative measurement unit selected as a surrogate of the level of activity. Output measures may be based on an input (for example, a purchase requirement for the purchasing activity) or an output (for example, a purchase order for the purchasing activity) of the activity considered to drive the activity cost in a linear way.

Activity unit: The heading under which a group of related activities is grouped. Also known as a budget subject.

Actual cost: Amounts determined on the basis of costs incurred (historical costs), as distinguished from predicted or forecasted costs.

Aggregation: The process of combining activities into functions.

Attributes: Qualitative data that can be counted for recording and analysis.

Back flushing: A costing system that first focuses on the throughput of an organization and then works backward when allocating costs between cost of goods sold and inventory.

Bill of activities (BOA): A list of activities required to manufacture a product.

Bill of material (BOM): A list of direct materials needed for the production of a given product.

Book value: Original cost less any accumulated depreciation.

Budget: The quantification of the operating plan in monetary units.

Budgeted cost: A cost that reflects management's opinion regarding future financial circumstances.

Burden rate: See *Overhead rate*.

Business process: An orderly arrangement of activities operating under a set of procedures in order to accomplish specific objectives.

Business rule: A rule that defines the goals, strategies, and regulations governing the industry.

By-product: See *Joint product*.

Capacity: The measured ability to produce: the amount of labor or machine time needed to meet a schedule.

Capital budgeting: The making of long-term planning decisions for investments and their financing.

Cause: A source event or factor that impacts subsequent events or activities.

Changeover: A partial set-up in which not all procedures are required.

Chart of accounts: A list of accounts maintained by a specific enterprise.

Contribution margin: Equal to revenue (sales) minus all variable expenses.

Control: (1) Action that implements the planning decision. (2) Performance evaluation that provides feedback of the results.

Conversion costs: Direct labor costs and factory overhead.

Cost: Resources sacrificed or forgone to achieve a specific objective.

Cost accounting system: The system in an organization that provides for the collection and assignment of costs to intermediate and final cost objects.

Cost accumulation: Collection of cost data in an organized way via an accounting system.

Cost allocation: The assignment and reassignment of a cost or group of costs to one or more cost objectives. Terms with assorted shades of meaning are cost relocation, cost assignment, cost apportionment, cost reapportionment, cost distribution, cost redistribution, cost tracing, and cost retracing.

Cost allocation base: A systematic means of relating a given cost or cost pool to a cost objective.

Cost apportionment: See *Cost allocation*.

Cost assignment: See *Cost allocation*.

Cost behavior pattern: Estimation of how costs behave as volume changes over a relevant range of activity levels.

Cost center: The smallest unit of an organization for which budgeted or actual costs are collected and which has some common characteristics for measuring performance and assigning responsibility. A cost center can consist of one or more work centers, work cells, or workstations.

Cost driver: A factor whose occurrence creates cost. The factor represents a prime cause of the level of activity (for example, the number of active components for production planning and control, inventory management, vendor contracting, and so on).

Cost elements: Types of costs (labor, material, service, supplies) associated with the manufacturing process.

Cost management: The management and control of activities to determine an accurate product cost, improve business processes, eliminate waste, identify cost drivers, plan operations, and set business strategies.

Cost pools: A grouping of costs caused by the same activity measure for the purpose of identification with or allocation to cost centers, processes, or products.

Critical success factors: Those factors deemed essential for the success of an organization.

Current cost: The cost of purchasing a currently held asset if an identical asset were purchased today; also, the cost of purchasing the services provided by that asset if identical assets cannot currently be purchased.

Customer: The recipient of a product or service.

Cycle time: The amount of time between the point when material for a product enters a factory and the point when the product is shipped.

Decomposition: The process of breaking down an activity into tasks.

Delphi method: The identification of departmental costs and activities via interviews with department heads.

Direct activity: An activity that can be traced to an output or service.

Direct cost: A cost item that can be identified specifically with a single cost object in an economically feasible manner. A direct cost is applied to the cost objective based on the actual content of the resource consumed by the cost objective. For example, a product that requires five man hours costing $20 per hour is charged $100, whereas a product that requires two man hours is charged $40.

Direct labor: The cost of labor that can be identified with a specific product.

Direct materials: Acquisition costs of all materials that are identified as part of the finished goods and may be traced to the finished goods in an economically feasible manner.

Driver: An activity or condition that has a direct influence on the operational performance and/or cost structure of other activities.

Effectiveness: The degree to which a predetermined objective or target is met.

Efficiency: The degree to which inputs are used in relation to a given level of outputs.

Engineered cost: Cost that results specifically from a clear-cut, measured relationship between inputs and outputs.

Environment: Set of uncontrollable factors that affect the success of a process.

Event: An occurrence. Also called state, state of nature.

Excellence: The cost-effective integration of activities within all units of an organization to continually improve the delivery of products and services to satisfy the customer.

Factors of production: All costs including labor, technology, utilities, travel, and so on.

Factory overhead: All costs other than direct material costs and direct labor costs that are associated with the manufacturing process. Also called factory burden, indirect manufacturing costs, manufacturing expenses, and manufacturing overhead.

Feedback: In control systems, consists of a comparison of the budget with actual results.

Financial accounting: External reporting, emphasizes the historical, custodial, and stewardship aspects of accounting. Heavily constrained by generally accepted accounting principles.

Fixed assets: Noncurrent, nonmonetary, tangible assets used in normal operations of a business.

Fixed cost: (1) Operating costs that do not vary with changes in the level of activity over a relevant range of such activity. (2) Those costs that will be unaffected by variations in activity level in a given period.

Function: A group of activities having a common objective within a business.

Full cost: Absorption cost plus an allocation of sales and administration cost. Also called fully distributed cost, fully allocated cost.

Gross margin: Excess of sales over the inventory cost of the goods sold. Also called gross profit.

Homogeneous cost: Cost in which each activity included has the same or a similar cause-and-effect relationship to a cost objective.

Indirect activities: Activities that are not directly attributable to a product or service.

Indirect costs: (1) Costs common to a multiple set of cost objectives and not directly assignable to such objectives in a specific time period. Such costs are usually allocated by systematic and consistent techniques to products, processes, or time periods. (2) Costs that are not directly assignable/traceable to a product or process. (3) Expenses that do not have a close causal relation with the items being produced. These costs do not include the cost of service departments. An example of an indirect cost is production supplies not included in the bill of material.

Indirect labor costs: All factory wages other than for direct labor.

Indirect manufacturing costs: All costs other than direct materials and direct labor that are associated with the manufacturing process. Also called factory burden, factory overhead, manufacturing expenses, and manufacturing overhead.

Input: The physical documents that trigger an activity.

Investment management: Part of a product's process planning and development activity, because it directly affects the selection and acquisition of the technology used to make the product.

JIT: See *Just in time*.

Just in time (JIT): System whereby each component on a production line is produced immediately as needed by the next step in the production line. Abbreviated as JIT production. A logistics approach designed to result in minimum inventory and waste during the manufacturing process.

JIT costing: Hybrid costing used in conjunction with just-in-time production systems.

Job order: Basic document used by job order costing to apply product costs. Also called job cost record and job cost sheet.

Job order costing: System used by organizations whose products or services are readily identified by individual units or batches, each of which receives varying inputs of direct materials, direct labor, and factory overhead.

Joint cost: Cost of a single process that yields two or more products (or services) simultaneously.

Joint products: Two or more products that (1) have relatively significant sales values and (2) are not separately identifiable as individual products until their split-off point.

Lead time: The span of time between the request for delivery of parts and their actual arrival.

Life-cycle costing: Accumulation of costs for activities that occur over the entire life cycle of a product, from inception to abandonment by the manufacturer and the consumer.

Machine hours: The measurement of time used by a machine to monitor specified levels of output.

Make/buy decision: The act of deciding whether to produce an item in-house or buy it from an outside vendor.

Management accounting: Identification, measurement, accumulation, analysis, preparation, interpretation, and communication of information that assists executives in fulfilling organizational objectives. Also called internal accounting.

Management information systems (MIS): An organizer's method of providing past, present, and prospective information relating to internal operations and external intelligence. It supports the planning, controlling, and operational functions of an organization by providing information in the proper time frame to assist decision makers.

Manufacturing: Transformation of materials into other goods through the use of labor and factory facilities.

Market research: The collection and interpretation of information about markets, market trends, and customer preferences.

Materials management: The function that regulates the movement of raw materials, supplies, and finished goods through the plant.

MIS: See *Management information system.*

Natural expense category: The basic classifications of cost that are universal and company-independent.

Non–value added cost: A cost or activity other than the *minimum* amount of equipment, materials, parts, space, and workers' time that is *absolutely essential* to *add value* to the enterprise.

Operation: The smallest unit of work used for planning or control purposes.

Operations: Manufacturing activities in which work is performed on parts.

Organization structure: The arrangement of lines of responsibility within the organization.

Output: The product of an activity. It is what users receive or what people produce.

Overhead cost: Cost other than direct cost.

Overhead rate: The percentage rate at which overhead is applied to products.

Overtime premium: Cost of the wages paid to all factory workers (for both direct labor and indirect labor) in excess of their straight line wage rates. Overtime premium is usually considered a part of overhead.

Performance driver: The prime factor influencing the performance of an activity (for example, the modularity of a product design on assembly lead time).

Period costs: Costs always expensed in the same period in which they are incurred; they do not go through an inventory stage.

Planned cost: A cost derived from the strategic and operational planning systems.

Planning: Delineation of goals, predictions of potential results of various ways of achieving goals, and a decision of how to attain the desired results.

Prime costs: Consist of direct materials cost plus direct labor costs.

Process: A combination of people, technology, raw materials, methods, and environment that produces a given product or service.

Process costing: System of applying costs to like products that are mass-produced in continuous fashion through a series of production steps called processes.

Product costs: Costs, including costs for raw materials, direct labor, and technology, that are directly or indirectly involved in the production of goods and services for sale to customers. Indirect costs include such items as equipment maintenance, factory utilities, and wages for facilitating services in the plant. Indirect costs are customarily assigned to products or services by an appropriate allocation technique.

Product development: All activities required to define, design, develop, test, release, and maintain the complete description of the products to be manufactured.

Production lead time: Time from the first stage of production to when the finished good comes off the production line.

Production planning and control system: A system that ensures a balance between resources and activities.

Profit center: Responsibility center that is accountable for costs and revenues.

Profit velocity: The ratio of product profit to production lead time.

Project: Complex job that often takes months or years to complete and requires the work of many different departments, divisions, or subcontractors.

Project management: Scheduling and organizational activities to control production.

Quality: Conformance of a product or service with a specified and direct labor. See also *Sales-quantity variance*.

Quality control activities: Checking, physical inspection, gauging, and testing done with the product.

Resources: Factors of production such as labor, technology, and materials.

Responsibility accounting: System that measures the plans and actions of each responsibility center.

Service: A type of output from an activity.

Service/support center: A work center whose primary mission is to provide specialized support to other departments.

Set-up: The process of preparing a machine or work center the first time for a manufacturing process.

Standard cost: Normally, the annual process of calculating the anticipated cost of a specific product at a given level of volume and under an assumed set of circumstances.

Strategic planning: A planning process that summarizes and articulates the basic operational tasks, objectives, goals, and strategies for the organization.

Sunk costs: Costs that have been incurred, but not consumed, for generating future revenue.

Target cost: A market-based cost that is calculated using a sales price necessary to capture a predetermined market share.

$$\text{Target cost} = \text{Sales price (for the target market share)} - \text{Desired profit}$$

Task: Work element of an activity.

Technology cost: The purchase price, start-up cost, interest, current market value adjustment, and risk premium of an acquisition.

Throughput: The total time of production through a facility (machine, work center, department, plant).

Time charging: A reporting system that tracks labor by task and flags shortfalls due to absences.

Total quality management: A management strategy in which all business functions work together to build quality into the products.

TQM: See *Total quality management.*

Tracing: The process of establishing a cause-and-effect relationship.

Transaction: Physical (including electronic) documents associated with activities that impact information.

Transfer price: Price charged by one segment (subunit, department, division, and so on) of an organization for a product or service supplied to another segment of the same organization.

Value added cost: The incremental cost of an activity to complete a required task at the lowest overall cost.

Variable cost: (1) A cost that increases as the volume of activity increases and decreases as the volume of activity decreases. (2) Those costs that are affected by the level of activity in a period.

Waste: The net total process output minus good process output.

Whole life cost: The cost to the customer from product inception to abandonment.

WIP: See *Work in progress.*

Work center: A specific area of the factory or company consisting of one or more people or machines that perform essentially the same function or can be treated the same. A work center may consist of one or more work cells or work stations.

Work in progress (WIP): The investment in goods in the process of being produced.

Work measurement: Careful analysis of a task, its size, the method used in its performance, and its efficiency. The objective of work measurement is to determine the work load in an operation and the number of workers needed to perform that work efficiently.

INDEX